Feng Shui

The Living Earth Manual

Other Feng Shui Books
by Stephen Skinner

Feng Shui
The Living Earth Manual

Stephen Skinner

TUTTLE PUBLISHING
Tokyo · Rutland, Vermont · Singapore

Published by Tuttle Publishing, an imprint of Periplus Editions (HK) Ltd., with editorial offices at 364 Innovation Drive, North Clarendon, Vermont 05759 U.S.A.

Library of Congress Cataloging-in-Publication Data
Skinner, Stephen, 1948–
 Feng shui : the living earth manual / Stephen Skinner.
  p. cm.
 Rev. ed. of: Living earth manual of feng-shui. 1982.
 Includes bibliographical references and index.
 ISBN 0-8048-3758-9 (pbk.)
 1. Feng shui. I. Skinner, Stephen, 1948– Living earth manual of feng-shui.
II. Title.
BF1779.F4S58 2006
133.3'337—dc22

                                                    2006024953

ISBN-10: 0-8048-3758-9
ISBN-13: 978-0-8048-3758-3

Distributed by:

**North America, Latin America
& Europe**
Tuttle Publishing
364 Innovation Drive
North Clarendon, VT 05759-9436 U.S.A.
Tel: 1 (802) 773-8930
Fax: 1 (802) 773-6993
info@tuttlepublishing.com
www.tuttlepublishing.com

Asia Pacific
Berkeley Books Pte. Ltd.
130 Joo Seng Road #06-01
Singapore 368357
Tel: (65) 6280-1330
Fax: (65) 6280-6290
inquiries@periplus.com.sg
www.periplus.com

First edition
10 09 08 07 06   10 9 8 7 6 5 4 3 2 1

Printed in Canada

TUTTLE PUBLISHING® is a registered trademark of Tuttle Publishing, a division of Periplus Editions (HK) Ltd.

Contents

Illustrations

Acknowledgments

My thanks to Bob Lawlor who first indicated the existence of feng shui to me, and to Helenc Hodge, who put up with me while I researched the subject.

I also wish to acknowledge the aid of the librarians at the British Library, the Warburg Institute, the Wellcome Library and especially the University of London's School of Oriental and African Studies (SOAS). My thanks also to John and Françoise Nicholas who were always very helpful, and for their hospitality in Hong Kong, where many of the last practitioners of this ancient art still carry on a flourishing trade. Together with Beth McKillop, they helped me with materials only to be found in Chinese.

My especial thanks to Nick Tereshchenko who gave me my first Ch'ing Dynasty feng shui *lo p'an*, to Beverly Lawton and Lindsay Roberts who typed the first manuscript, and to Evelyn Lip for her help while I was in Singapore.

The drawing of the dragon and tiger schema by J. Bryant is reproduced by permission from the *Annals of the Association of American Geographers*, vol. 64, no. 4, 1974, p. 509, fig. 2, Chuen-yan David Lai. The drawing of the full *lo p'an* is used as an illustration by J. J. M. De Groot in *The Religious System of China*, Brill, Leiden, 1897.

Early Chinese sources include the map of a *hsueh* from the *Luan t'ou chih mi*, vol. 4. The illustration showing the use of the feng shui compass in the Ch'ing Dynasty appeared first in *Shao Kao*. The elemental forms of the mountains are attributed to Kuo P'o in his classic *Ts'ui t'ien hsuan nu ch'ing-nang hai-chiao ching*, and the forms of the nine flying stars appeared in the *Ti-li ta-cheng*, vol. I. The river formation is drawn from the *Shui-lung ching*, the "Water Dragon Classic."

The Chinese house plans are reprinted with the permission of the publishers from *Under the Ancestors' Shadow* by

Francis L. K. Hsu, Stanford University Press, copyright of 1948 and 1967 by Francis L. K. Hsu; and *Chinese Houses* by Ronald Knapp, Tuttle Publishing.

The author and publisher wish to thank the Hong Kong Government Information Service and the *South China Morning Post* for their helpful cooperation.

Also thanks to Jin Peh for proofreading the revised edition and to Er Choon Haw for keying the Chinese characters.

Preface to the Second Edition

A lot has changed since I first wrote this book, and accordingly a lot of additional material has been added to this edition. My views and understanding of feng shui have not so much changed as expanded.

When I first wrote this book back in 1976, I did not dream that feng shui would take off in the West in the way it has in the past twenty years. For me it was the satisfaction of putting down on paper an intriguing subject that I had pieced together from conversations with feng shui masters in Hong Kong, from old Chinese texts in SOAS, from Joseph Needham's pioneering work on the history of Chinese science, and from the scattered but biased mentions made of the practice by missionaries in the nineteenth century.

In fact, it seemed in those days as if even the Chinese I spoke to were not particularly that interested in the subject. I saw a beautiful, complex, and functional system, that overlapped my interests and profession of geography lecturer, going to waste.

The original book devoted sixty pages each to the two main schools of feng shui, Form and Compass, with a little bit about interior household feng shui added at the end. In fact it was household feng shui that caught the imagination of the West in the 1980s and 1990s.

This new edition leaves much of the material on Compass* and Form School feng shui untouched. I am happy to discover that despite thirty years of further study of this fascinating subject I do not feel that much that I wrote in 1976 needs amendment. I have however added more material to these chapters. The household feng shui chapter has been considerably amplified, especially in showing the way Eight Mansion feng shui integrates with the rest of feng shui practice.

---

* A forthcoming book by me devoted entirely to the compass, or *lo p'an*, will take this material a lot further.

There is no point in my adding Flying Star or other formulas for household feng shui to the third section, as these have been written about extensively in other books both by me and other authors over the past decade or so.

The original 1976 edition came with an extensive bibliography of Chinese texts, as that was all that was really available, but the publisher of the 1982 edition chose to omit these as too complicated.

I trust that this reissue of the text, which could justly be described as the "book that started it all" at least in the Western world, is welcomed by you, the reader.

Stephen Skinner
Johor Bahru
www.SSkinner.com

Etymological Note on Feng Shui

Geomancy is really a misnomer for the Chinese practice of feng shui, as this word more properly relates to an Arab form of divination that spread north into Europe and south into Africa at the end of the first millennium. The word *geomancy* was, however, adopted by the Reverend Yates in 1870 to translate *feng shui*. The present work is concerned with feng shui, the location of *ch'i*, dragon veins of energy in the earth, and their interaction with man as part of his subtle environment.

Feng shui has been used in preference to geomancy to describe this ancient Chinese art throughout this book. Its completely unrelated namesake, divinatory geomancy, has been the subject of two previous books by the present author. In these books (see Bibliography) he traces the history of divinatory geomancy in Africa and Europe and Madagascar, demonstrating that there is no cultural contact or similarity of method or objectives between feng shui and divinatory geomancy.

Although feng shui (wind and water) is the most often found and most colloquial Chinese name for the Chinese theory and practice of siting, the name that is most consistently used in classical Chinese texts is *ti li* (literally "land patterns," which is translated in modern times as "geography"). This emphasizes the fact that the ancient Chinese saw feng shui not so much as a superstitious practice by itself, but as an integral part of the study of the land itself and the patterns on it, both natural and man-made. Because of this linguistic crossover, my curiosity as a geographer made me immediately interested in the subject.

A third and perhaps older term is *kan-yu*, which literally means "cover and support," or even "cover and chariot," referring to the Heaven and the Earth. It encompasses the old resonance theories of traditional Taoist philosophy, which held that actions on Earth affect the Heavens and movements in the Heavens act upon the surface of the Earth. Indeed, a lot of feng shui is concerned with mapping these interactions.

Although in the great Chinese encyclopedias feng shui is listed under the *kan-yu* chapter, it is likely that originally the two practices were quite distinct. I think that *kan-yu* was possibly the original designation of the Compass School, while *ti li* and feng shui were probably the early designation of the Form School. It is only in later years that the distinction has become somewhat muddied, although it still survives in Taiwan.

Just taken literally, *kan-yu* with its meaning "chariot of Heaven and Earth" might be seen to refer to the round Plate of the compass (Heaven) set into the square Earth Plate of its holder (a feature that many decorative *lo p'ans* now lack), while feng shui refers, obviously, to the natural elements that would be more the concern of the Form School.

Steven J. Bennett in his article "Patterns of the Sky and the Earth: the Chinese science of applied cosmology" in *Chinese Science* (1978, 3: 1–26) prefers to call feng shui "astroecology," which sounds rather too modern and doesn't cover many of the aspects of feng shui.

Bennett also likes to refer to it as "siting theory," which gives it a rather geographical flavor. Feng shui is however much more than theory. It is definitely not a system of ecology, despite whatever its New Age proponents believe. It is also not a system of spirituality, except inasmuch as some of its practices, especially where they relate to the dead, shade into Taoist practice. It is definitely not a part of Buddhism, as one prominent American proponent would have you believe, although it has been used by Buddhists in the construction of their temples. It is, however, an intensely practical approach to the modification of luck, based upon an understanding of location, direction, *ch'i* energy, and landform that has yet to be achieved in the West. Luck is seen, by the practitioners of feng shui, as a commodity that can be hoarded, increased, or lost rather than merely a one-time lottery win.

Introduction

The ancient Chinese art of feng shui lies behind the whole pattern of the Chinese landscape. It is an attitude to the life in the land that has enabled China to feed one of the densest populations in the world without doing too great violence to the Earth.

Although China is a predominantly agricultural country, the Chinese art of living within the rhythms of the land and the seasons is just as applicable to life in the Western world. Although the system of feng shui is intrinsically linked to traditional Chinese Taoist philosophy, the practical tenets are universal.

Just as acupuncture measures and corrects the life force in man, so can feng shui cultivate the life force or *ch'i* in the earth for his benefit.

Ch'i flows through the earth like an underground stream that varies its course according to the seasons and to changes made by nature or man to the surface of the Earth. The underground streams that can be observed during caving expeditions are not the same as the channels that carry *ch'i*. A parallel can be drawn with the flow of *ch'i* through the acupuncture meridians of the body. These meridians are not the same as the blood vessels that can be dissected by the surgeon's knife, but convey life energy through their own specific and precisely locatable channels.

Nevertheless the effectiveness of acupuncture has been admirably demonstrated to the satisfaction of Western medical practitioners on numerous occasions. According to the practitioners of acupuncture, their work relies upon locating these, as yet undetected, meridians and modifying the flow of *ch'i* through them.

To complete the parallel, the practitioners of feng shui manipulate the surface of the body of the Earth, and the positioning of buildings, ponds, and so on, to influence the flow of *ch'i* along its hidden veins or dragon lines. The feng shui expert is therefore commonly referred to as a *lung kia* or "dragon man," as he traces or "rides" these veins of *ch'i* from their source high in the mountains (the mythical abode of dragons) to the lower slopes where they affect for good or ill the people living on or near them.

Consequently the art of feng shui consists in trapping and pooling beneficial *ch'i* and deflecting malefic *ch'i* from the site chosen. The pooling of good *ch'i* brings not just agricultural fertility but a fertility of the environment, a locale suitable for living free of the background of unease often associated with quarters in cities, suburbs, or individual dwellings built contrary to the prevailing flow of life in the land, or whose "atmosphere" has been muddied by conflict both human and natural.

Such conditions can often be restored to peace by the manipulation of the environment by a "dragon man"; as, by analogy, a body can be restored to health by the regularization of the acupuncture meridians.

The parallel between the body and the earth hasn't been chosen as an arbitrary metaphor but reflects the Chinese view of the wholeness of the universe not divided rigidly into the categories of Western theology (matter and spirit) or science (living and dead). Instead the "dragon man" looks upon existence as a continuum, much as C. G. Jung saw the universe: the external macrocosmic world being reflected in, and acting upon, the internal microcosmic world.

After all, who can deny that adjustment of the environment, by methods no more esoteric than the addition of landscaped parklands to a city or the decoration and refurnishing of a room, reflect directly upon the lives of the inhabitants?

The rules of feng shui apply equally to the siting of a whole city, or even a province, down to the arrangement of the living space in the smallest studio apartment in the heart of that city.

Form Feng Shui— *Luan t'ou*

I

Wind and Water: What Is Feng Shui?

To be in the right place facing the right direction doing the right thing at the right time is, then, a cross between being practically efficient and being ritually correct. It is being in tune with the universe.

—Stephan Feuchtwang

Many look for their Shangri-la on the surface of the Earth, others voyage within for illumination. The ancient Chinese art of feng shui combines the axes of both quests, declaring that what you make of your location and environment on the face of the Earth also affects your interior peace, effectiveness, and luck. The formulas of feng shui rely upon locating and harnessing the "dragon lines" of energy that pass through the earth, affecting the quality of life upon its surface in varying degrees.

Popular Chinese religion, based on Taoism, is centered on ancestor worship and a veneration of various spirits of a place, not unlike early Greek beliefs. In China these were overlaid by other more abstract philosophies while the original beliefs still retained their strength among those closest to the soil. In Greece these early animistic beliefs helped generate the later complex mythologies that were the basis of the classical roots of European culture. Chinese animistic beliefs spawned the various observances and practices such as feng shui that are unique to China, but they also prompted scientific exploration of energies that are every bit as concrete as radio waves, but have yet to be identified by western science. Just as the Chinese discovered and used the principles of the magnetic compass 1500 years before they were understood in Europe, so Western science lags a long way behind in the recognition and utilization of energies such as *ch'i*.

The landscape teamed with life: demons, guardians, and spirits of mountains, pools, springs, trees, and rocks, in fact of any prominent feature of a locality. All of these could become objects for veneration, fear, or placation. Life was not confined merely to that defined as living by biology, but pulsed through the rocks, waters, earth, and winds. The whole universe was seen as a living organism.

Chinese art depicts this feel for the spirits of the land and portrays one or two salient features, which live and breathe to the exclusion of all else, often in splendid isolation in space or cloud. Western art fills in all the background, with a passion for leaving no empty space. Similarly, Western architecture is hell-bent on fitting in as much as possible into a nice neat rectangular grid that is carved into the ground by bulldozers: it takes no care with the siting of each unit, cuts out any clusters of unique, eccentric, or erratic buildings, and emphasizes only the practical, never the beautiful: such is its formula. The Chinese, however, could no more build houses or villages that cut unthinkingly into the flesh of the landscape than would a surgeon operate without looking first at the patient's body.

It is nevertheless easy for Western "developers" to slash their way across the countryside in the name of the great god "Motorway" or create new towns without any more thought to the underlying land than is required by their plumbers.

To add to the landscape one must create not a thorn in its flesh but a form that flows and breathes with the rhythm of the earth in which it is planted. Wood and stone taken from nature are to be hewed and fitted back into nature. Pagodas, houses, temples, towns, or hamlets in China are all part of the Earth and were built as such. It is only since the Revolution of 1911 and the consequent industrialization of China that synthetic materials and discordant forms and shapes have grown up. Only since then has function or productivity taken priority over peace and harmony with the living land. In 1927 feng shui was suppressed in China itself, and so ever since then, with a rush in the middle of the twentieth century and again in 1966–76, masters of feng shui have migrated to Taiwan,

Hong Kong, or Southeast Asia. The strange result of this is that today the great masters of feng shui are to be found in these countries not in China, their origin.

The art of living in harmony with the land and deriving the greatest benefit, peace, and prosperity from being in the right place at the right time is called feng shui. *Feng* (wind) and *Shui* (water) together make up *feng shui* (pronounced "foong-shway" in Mandarin but more like "fun-sooee" in Cantonese). Together they express the power of the flowing elements of the natural environment, and this power is expressed in, and derived from, the flow of energy not only on the surface, which has been sculpted by wind and water, but also through the earth. Placing oneself in a properly planned and favorable feng shui environment will bring good fortune, peace, fertility, and a longer life.

Often people who do not know why it is so, feel "at home" in one environment but not in another. Apart from the obvious environmental factors such as type of house or neighbors, there are also the more subtle effects of the interaction of that person with the feng shui environment. Where in new developments there is a feeling of bareness and sterility, it is because the wound caused in nature by the developers has not had time to heal over. Where the violence done to nature is great, or the elements introduced so out of accord with the landscape, the wound will never heal. Many large Western cities, particularly their more modern sections, have done so much violence to the underlying earth that it is doubtful if it will ever "accept" the new structures, perhaps not until they lie in ruins and nature has again claimed them. Ruins often induce a kind of melancholic euphoria, at least if one visits them alone.

During the nineteenth and twentieth centuries, Europeans in China came up against the phenomenon of feng shui. The Chinese regard for feng shui forced missionaries to remove the tops of their church spires and railway builders to change the course of their tracks, in accordance with the Chinese interpretation of the balance of the hidden forces in the landscape. One Chinese syndicate actually bought a length of track simply to destroy it and its adverse effect on the feng shui of its district.

The inherent Chinese belief in feng shui was so unquestioned that many of the early clashes left the Chinese bewildered that the "foreign devils" who wished to build spires, railways, and other incongruously straight structures should be so ignorant of the basic principles of nature.

Historically China has always looked upon itself as the well-balanced "Middle Kingdom," the center of the habitable world. A consistent foreign policy of several millennia that cut China off from the rest of the world has reinforced this view, only in the past few decades being consciously broken down at the political level.

A naive result of this is that traditional Chinese geography insisted that all rivers flowed eastward (as indeed most do in China), and also that all the highest mountains, the source of the rivers, were located in the west. In the sense that Mount Everest is west of China they are of course right. Additionally, this formalized geography pictured the south as the quarter of the greatest warmth and hence of the greatest good, while most of the cold winds (*feng*) blew from the dark north.

Accordingly all Chinese maps were oriented with the quarter of greatest goodness, the south, logically at the top of the page. We will follow this convention (the opposite of Western cartographic procedure), identifying north at the bottom of the page, east on the left and west on the right. Although this takes some getting used to, there are some symbolic benefits to thinking in the Chinese mode and it certainly makes the comprehension of feng shui texts significantly easier.

So, from the position of the viewer in the north, the world, city, or site under consideration is oriented as shown in Figure 1. Given this orientation, and apart from the rules of feng shui, it is common sense to protect one's habitation from the bitter winter winds of the north, and encourage the balmy airs of summer and the south. If prosperity was ever linked with health, then the theory behind feng shui certainly has a factual enough foundation in China!

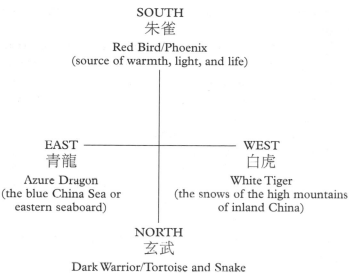

SOUTH
朱雀
Red Bird/Phoenix
(source of warmth, light, and life)

EAST ——————————————— WEST
青龍　　　　　　　　　　　白虎

Azure Dragon
(the blue China Sea or
eastern seaboard)

White Tiger
(the snows of the high mountains
of inland China)

NORTH
玄武
Dark Warrior/Tortoise and Snake
(the cold, dark northern plains)

*Figure 1. Orientation of the site and relationship between the
Celestial Animal symbols of the cardinal points of the compass*

AZURE DRAGON

WHITE TIGER

RED BIRD

BLACK TURTLE

Figure 2. The four Celestial Animals

Following the Hermetic convention of "as above, so below," Chinese geographers identified the basic regions of their country with the various constellations of the night sky said to rule them. This identification is in fact still reflected on one ring of the traditional Chinese compass, or *lo p'an*. Obviously this creates some overlap between astronomy, geography (*ti li*), and feng shui, inevitable in a system that sees mutual interaction as an essential feature of a living universe. Within this theoretical framework are to be found a number of practical, sociological, siting, and even sanitary considerations (such as are not far removed from the minds of modern city planners).

The macrocosmic view of the interrelation of the constellations and the geography of the whole Chinese empire is reflected in the more pragmatic approach to the effects of certain stars upon towns or individual dwellings. From early descriptions it has been ascertained that the as yet unopened tomb of the first emperor, Ch'in Shih Huang Ti, embodies this thinking, with a floor made to represent the whole empire of China, with rivers made of mercury, and a ceiling painted with the constellations of the night sky.

Table 1. Macrocosmic and microcosmic siting of the living and the dead

Yang chai (houses) location of the living	*Yin chai* (tombs) location of ancestors
Macrocosmic Country or empire City or town House	Tombs of the emperors Clan temples Tomb
Microcosmic Orientation of the rooms of the house	Orientation of the gravestone

Yin and Yang Dwellings

Dwellings are divided into those of the living (houses) and those of the dead (graves and tombs), for the Chinese see no break between the living and the dead in terms of family or ancestral relationships.

At the same time there is a microcosmic/macrocosmic axis to consider, so that the field of action of feng shui can be laid out as shown in Table 1. Although much of the available feng shui lore concerns the *yin chai* (陰宅), or grave locations, most of these rules can also be extrapolated to explain the intricacies of *yang chai* (陽宅), or house siting. Likewise the rules for city orientation are also of use in the siting of individual houses.

The Two Schools of Feng Shui

Superimposed on this classification are the two main schools of thought in feng shui, the Form School (*luan t'ou*) and the Compass School (*li ch'i*). The former and the older of the two is concerned with the visible form of the landscape surrounding the site under consideration, be it a *yang chai* (house) or a *yin chai* (tomb). The Compass School, however, is concerned with a time axis and a complex set of relationships between "sensitive" directions as indicated by an elaborate, many ringed Chinese compass called a *lo p'an*.

It is fashionable nowadays to point out that the main schools of feng shui are the San He, San Yuan, and Hsuan Kung schools, and that Form and Compass are not the actual names of schools. While this is true, they represent an easy division of the two main ways in which feng shui has been practiced. Both schools of course use the compass, or *lo p'an*, to indicate direction, but the Form School is more interested in the surrounding landscape of mountains and rivers, while the Compass School is more concerned with the division of the "feng shui horizon" into smaller and smaller divisions, as shown on the *lo p'an*.

If you want to use the formal Chinese school names, then San He doctrines tend to concentrate on Form, while San Yuan doctrines require detailed study of the compass and very precise readings of that instrument.

Each of the two schools has a number of names, the most common of which are:

1. Form and Configuration School (*hsing shih,* 形勢), is also known as:
   - Mountain Peaks and Vital Embodiment School (*luan t'ou,* 巒頭)
   - Shapes School
   - Kanchow [Ganzhou] method
   - Kiangsi [Jiangxi] method (this being an indication of its geographical origins and the dwelling place of its patriarch, Yang Yun Sung).

   The Form and Configuration School flourished in the Kiangsi [Jiangxi] and Anhui provinces (famous for its mountains), but is now primarily practiced in Taiwan.

2. Compass School is also referred to as:
   - Directions and Positions School (*fang wei,* 方位)
   - *Ch'i* Pattern School (*li ch'i,* 理氣)
   - Fukien [Fujian] School (its probable province of origin and home of Wang Chih, one of its early major proponents)
   - Method of Man
   - Houses and Dwellings Method
   - Ancestral Hall Method (*tsung miao chih fa*)
   - Min School

   The Compass School flourished in Fukien [Fujian] and Chekiang [Zhejiang] provinces, but is now predominantly in Taiwan, Singapore, Malaysia, and Hong Kong.

By the late nineteenth and early twentieth centuries, the two schools were no longer separate and distinct. Feng shui men practiced both methods of siting in both Fukien [Fujian] and Kiangsi [Jiangxi], according to De Groot, but they maintained that there was still a clear demarcation between the two techniques. Obviously the mountainous areas of the south such as Kwangsi [Guangxi] are more susceptible to Form School interpretation, while those who lived on the flat plains needed the compass (*lo p'an*) to detect favorable directions in an otherwise unremarkable and featureless landscape.

The Form School: Yang Yun Sung

Yang Yun Sung (or Shuh-Meu as he is sometimes called, c. AD 840–c. 888) was an Imperial feng shui master, or *hsiensheng* (先生), to the emperor from AD 874–888 and a native of Kwangsi [Guangxi] province, who spent most of this life in Kiangsi [Jiangxi]. Both from his widespread fame and the many works he wrote, he has always been regarded as the patriarch of the School of Forms, although its theory predated him by many centuries. He laid particular stress on the shape of mountains and the direction of watercourses, and the influences of the dragon that play a considerable part in his system under various names and aspects. His three best-known books are consequently concerned with dragons:

a. *Hun Lung Ching* or "Classic of the Art of Rousing the Dragon," sometimes referred to as the "Classic of the Moving or Shaking Dragon";
b. *Ch'ing-Nang Ao-Chih* or "Secret Meanings of the Universe";
c. *I Lung Ching* or "Canon for the Approximation of Dragons," which refers especially to those forms and outlines of nature where dragon and tiger do not prominently stand forth and are, as it were, concealed;
d. *Shih-Erh Chang-Fa* or "Method of the Twelve Stave Lines," which has become a classic for the determination of the *hsueh* or "lair" of the dragon in which it is most favorable to build or bury, is included in the *Ch'ing-Nang Ao-Chih*.

These are among the great classics of feng shui.

The Form School was the first to be formally established and is the most naturally based, taking into account the configuration of the surrounding landscape as seen from the site of the building or the grave.

Compass School: Wang Chih

Not until the rise of the Sung Dynasty (AD 960) were all the elements of feng shui gathered into one system, built firmly on a philosophical basis and developed methodically, so as to combine every form of influence that Heaven and Earth were supposed to have on human affairs. Based on the metaphysical speculations of the Sung Dynasty, a second school of feng shui arose that laid more particular stress upon the *kua*, the eight trigrams; the Heavenly Stems and Earthly Branches; and the twenty-eight Constellations (more of which later), assigning a place of minor importance to the actual configurations of the earth.

The chief representative of the Compass School, Wang Chih (also named Chao-khing or Khung-chang) spent the latter period of his life in the north of Fukien [Fujian] province, where he wrote his "Canon of the Core or Center" and his "Disquisition on the Queries and Answers," both of which were published by his pupil Yeh Shuh-liang.

The Ming Dynasty writer Wang Wei (1323–74) summarizes the position of the two schools and their background in the *Lung heng* as follows:

> The theories of the geomancers [sic] have their sources in the ancient yin-yang school. Although the ancients in establishing their cities and erecting their buildings always selected sites [by feng shui], the art of selecting burial sites originated with the *Tsang shu* ("Burial Book") in twenty parts, written by Kuo P'o of the Chin Dynasty . . . In later times those who practiced the art divided into two schools.
>
> One is called *tsung miao chih fa* [Compass School]. It began in Fukien [Fujian], and its origins go far back; with Wang Chih of the Sung Dynasty it gained currency. Its theory emphasizes the Planets and the Trigrams; a

yang hill should face in a yang direction, a yin hill in a yin direction, so they are not at odds. Exclusive reliance is put on the eight Trigrams and the five Planets, which are used to determine the principles of generation and destruction. The art is still preserved in Chekiang [Zhejiang], but very few people employ it.

The other is called the Kiangsi [Jiangxi] method [Form School]. It started with Yang Yun Sung and Tseng Wen-ti of Kanchou [Ganzhou], and its doctrine was refined especially by Lai Ta-yu and Hsieh-Tzu-i. Its theory emphasises landforms and terrain (*hsing shih*) taking them from where they arise to where they terminate, and thereby determining position and orientation. [Practitioners] give their whole attention to the mutual appropriateness of dragons, sites, eminences, and waters, obstinately refusing to discuss anything else. Nowadays [during the Ming Dynasty] south of the Yangtze, everyone follows it.

The Form School utilizes a greater degree of subjective insight while the Compass School, although more complex in its theory, is more objective and mechanical in application. As Chao Fang (in *Tsang shu wen ta*) expressed it:

In the Form School the principles are clear but the practice is difficult . . . with the Compass [School] the principles are obscure but the practice is easy.

The rationale of the manual for "yang dwellings" (homes) is by now apparent, but the reasons why graves should be sited with care according to feng shui principles is less obvious. Basically it is necessary to appreciate that for the Chinese the ancestor was a very important person and kinship and family group ties were much closer than those experienced in the West. Extended families or clans living together, often with three or more generations under the same roof, reinforced this attitude, so that the relocation of a grandparent was perhaps more important (when their status changed to that of dead ancestor) than was their location while they were living.

Furthermore, the more distinguished ancestors or clan leaders became objects of veneration, both to make sure that they continued to look with favor upon the living and because their status as spirits gave them considerable power over the fortunes, fate, and circumstances of their living descendants. This power of course was more specifically directed to blood-line relatives, consequently attention to the comforts of the ancestor was a most important part of Chinese life.

Oddly it was even thought that ancestors could be "manipulated," by giving their grave or tomb good feng shui, to benefit their descendants by the accumulation of *ch'i* whether the ancestors wished it or not.

A belief intrinsic in the system of ancestor veneration, which predates Taoism or Confucianism in China, is that (one of) the souls of ancestors are linked with the site of their tombs. As they also have a direct effect on the lives of their descendants, it follows logically that if their tombs are located favorably on the site of a strong concentration of earth energy, or *ch'i*, not only will they be happy but they will also derive the power to aid their descendants from the accumulated *ch'i* of the site. As the Reverend Eitel (1873:21) puts it:

The fortunes of the living depend in some measure upon the favorable situation of the tombs of their ancestors. If a tomb is so placed, that the animal spirit of the deceased, supposed to dwell there, is comfortable and free of disturbing elements, so that the soul has unrestricted egress and ingress, the ancestors' spirits will feel well disposed towards their descendants, will be enabled to constantly surround them, and willing to shower upon them all the blessings within reach of the spirit

world. So deeply ingrafted [sic] is this idea of the influence of the dead upon the living, that Chinese wishing
to get into the good graces of foreigners will actually go
out to the Hong Kong cemeteries in the Happy Valley,
and worship there at the tombs of foreigners, supposing
that the spirits of the dead there, pleased with their
offerings and worship, would influence the spirits of the
living, and thus produce a mutual good understanding
between all the parties concerned.

Consequently the art and science of feng shui is of prime
importance for locating the best-aspected site for a grave as
this decision affects the fortunes of all the deceased's children
and their families.

As Chinese belief included at least three spiritual principles, or souls, as well as the physical body, it was necessary
that each be laid to rest with the utmost care; one soul (*p'o*)
remains in the grave with the body, benefiting from the
hopefully good feng shui of the site, one in the ancestral
tablet of the household altar (by which link the benefits of
the feng shui of the burial site affect the family), and one soul
(*hun*) in the other world, purgatory or paradise, more or less
beyond the reach of feng shui influences

From John Blofeld's excellent Taoist work *Beyond the Gods*
comes a story that illustrates the intimate connection between
the soul in the grave, in this case suffering from an ill-
thought-out burial, and the soul in the ancestral tablets who
is free to roam the house and affect his descendants.

The other story . . . has been told me in all seriousness
by a Malayan Chinese student during our undergraduate
days at Cambridge. While still too young to comprehend
the fact of death, he was told by his parents that his
grandfather has passed away. It was hard for him to
understand why his daddy and mummy looked so

upset; for death, whatever that might mean, had not changed Grandfather in any special way; he was often to be seen wandering about the house at night, looking grumpy just as usual. But when his daddy came to hear of this, he grew dreadfully pale and said something like: "Alas, dear boy, your Gran must be in terrible distress, otherwise his restless spirit would have left this house forever. Next time you see him, be sure to ask."

Unafraid, the innocent child questioned his grandfather at their very next encounter.

"My boy, you can have no idea," replied the ghost. "I can find no rest at all. The gate-keepers of the Chinese heavens chase me away, declaring there is no admission for people dressed in European-style clothes like this white drill suit in which your father so thoughtlessly clothed my corpse. At the Christian heaven, it is the same. The guards drive me off because someone once forgot to sprinkle holy water on my forehead. Now nothing is left for me but to wander unendingly among those unhappy shades who, being childless, have no descendants to offer sacrifices before their tombs, which is really quite unfair considering I begat no less than seven sons. They do offer sacrifice, but I never get a whiff because the essence of the food and drink is wafted straight to heaven."

When the child reported this problem to his parents, the old man's body was hurriedly exhumed and the unsatisfactory white drill suit exchanged for a Chinese robe, whereafter the ghost was never seen again!

Ancestor veneration takes place on the first and fifteenth day of every lunar month as well as the anniversary of the death of the ancestor concerned. *Worship* is actually a misleading term as there is no thought that the ancestor has become a god (although some distinguished ancients did) but that filial duty or genuine affection is being expressed, and beyond that, the limited power of the ancestor to help or hinder his living descendants has to be propitiated or even pandered to.

The filial duty that partly motivates ancestor veneration is an extension of the Confucian ethics that became the basis for imperial law under which respect for elders, dead or alive, was a cardinal duty. Thus, not only was ancestor "worship" designed to promote the favor of the ancestor, but also to build up a supply of grace from regular application of this Confucian precept. This "worship" took the form of supplying the soul of the ancestor with the necessities that he required in life: food cooked and cut up is laid out with chopsticks and much kowtowing in front of the ancestral tablet. The tablet acts almost like a talisman for storing the soul of the ancestor. The ritual is carried out by the head of the family and for the benefit of the family.

One typically Chinese dread, exemplified in Blofeld's anecdote, is that their line of descendants will dry up and there will be no one to look after the needs of their soul. In this case the soul becomes a "hungry ghost" who is generally vindictive and preys on travelers. He may eventually need to be exorcized, like a demon, by a monk or priest.

The fear of neither being able to receive the ancestral offerings nor having any descendants to offer them is very real. Hence the importance of a good feng shui burial which leaves the *p'o* in a comfortable habitation and ensures that there are plenty of fortunate descendants to continue the worship and sustain the *hun* of the ancestor.

No less important is the selection of a site for the home of the living or the rearrangement of its rooms to improve its occupant's eventual happiness, health, and wealth.

2

Earth's Blood: *Ch'i*

The fraction of the Earth's magnetic field produced by outside sources is now understood to be an important representation of the electromagnetic activities in the Earth's upper atmosphere . . . the daily varying part of the Earth's magnetic field can be ascribed to electric currents flowing in the Earth's upper atmosphere.

—Article on the magnetic field of the Earth in *Encyclopedia Britannica*, vol. 6, 1974

Whichever school of thought is followed, the main objective is the clarification of the *ch'i* content of a site. *Ch'i* (氣) has no equivalent in Western terminology, except perhaps for the Hebrew *ruach*, which has been translated as "breath of life." *Ch'i* is the active energy that flows through the forms produced by *li*. As such, it is responsible for the changes in form that are a characteristic of all living beings, and that includes the Earth itself.

Ch'i acts at every level—on the human level it is the energy flowing through the acupuncture meridians of the body; at the agricultural level it is the force that, if not stagnant, brings fertile crops; and at the climatic level it is the energy carried on the winds and by the waters.

The various forms of *ch'i* include *sheng ch'i* (生氣), or vital/birth *ch'i*, and *ssu ch'i* (死氣), or torpid *ch'i*. The former is yang *ch'i* and the latter yin *ch'i*, so that *sheng ch'i* flows most readily during the hours of the rising sun (midnight to noon), while *ssu ch'i* prevails during the declining hours of the sun (from noon to midnight). As the sun moves from east to west, the compass points from which one can expect either *sheng ch'i* or *ssu ch'i* alternate. Just like the tides, *ch'i* ebbs and flows, not only throughout the day but also throughout the seasons of the year and within the framework of the sixty-year cycle upon which the Chinese calendar is based. Consequently determining the current state of *ch'i* flow, related both to the clock and the calendar, is important when beginning an enterprise, building, altering, moving, buying, or selling property. This is simply expressed by the "Dwelling Classic," which explains how important it is to act when there is a flow of vital *ch'i* that will energize the biosphere of the site:

> Every year has twelve months, and each month has positions in time and space of vital and torpid *ch'i*. Whenever one builds on a vital *ch'i* position of a month, wealth will come his way and accumulate . . . To violate a monthly position of torpid *ch'i* will bring bad luck and calamity.

The interrelation between time, space, and *ch'i* is explained in the "Dwelling Classic" in terms of combinations of the twelve Earthly Branches (*ti chih,* 地支) and the ten Heavenly Stems (*t'ien kan,* 天干) used to mark the passage of time. The twelve Earthly Branches mark the twelve double hours of the day and the twelve directions of the feng shui compass. Combined with the ten Heavenly Stems, they form the cycle of 120 *fen-chin*, which also caters for the sixty-day and sixty-year cycle of the Chinese calendar. (These terms are further explained in Chapter 4.)

Hence, there is a change in direction and quality of *ch'i* flow every two hours of the day. From the larger perspective each year of the sixty-year cycle has a different form of *ch'i*, and these *ch'i* flows are not repeated again exactly for the next sixty years. Consequently exact determination of the best starting time for any venture that might involve *ch'i*— and this extends to activities other than building—is quite an exacting science.

For the Compass School of feng shui the interaction of the Stems and Branches with time and space are very important.

However, the Form School thought of *ch'i* more in terms of its "pneumatic circulation" and looked upon the circulation of *ch'i* almost in the same way that the modern geographer looks upon the hydrologic cycle. Just as the water evaporates off the surface of oceans and rivers and ascends to the sky before condensing and falling again as rain to make those very rivers, so the circulation of *ch'i* fluctuates between Heaven and Earth. When vital *ch'i* is congealed or accumulated, it encourages growth of all kinds beneficial to mankind; where it is dispersed, there is barrenness; and where it has gone torpid, there is death and decay. Each is a natural phase in the circulation of *ch'i*, and it is for us to take advantage of this cycle just as the farmer takes advantage of the climatic changes through the year and plants crops in spring and reaps in autumn rather than attempting the reverse, which would of course be disastrous.

Just as a farmer might look for a spring of fresh water, so you can locate or encourage the welling up of *ch'i* from the ground. Such points occur where there is a change of landform, a bend in the river or the change from plain to scarp, or the meeting of a yang and a yin landform. In each case the natural node is marked by a sharp change from yin to yang, or vice versa.

To understand feng shui it is essential to appreciate *ch'i*. On a microcosmic level, *ch'i* is the energy of the body's breath, which, if concentrated in various parts of the body, can enable the practitioner to perform the more amazing feats of the Chinese martial arts schools.

What is true of the microcosm is also true of the macrocosm, and *ch'i* is naturally accumulated and may be enhanced at certain points in the earth by the application of landscape alterations made in accordance with feng shui rules.

In *Tao Magic*, Laszlo Legeza (1975, p. 13) explains *ch'i:*

Ch'i, the Vital Spirit, fills the world of the Taoist. It is the Cosmic Spirit which vitalizes and infuses all things, giving energy to man, life to nature, movement to water, growth to plants. It is exhaled by the mountains, where the spirits live, as clouds and mist and, therefore, the undulating movement of clouds, mist, or air filled with smoke rising from burning incense, is a characteristic mystic representation of *ch'i* in Taoist art.

Note the emphasis on clouds and mist, the feng and shui, forming dragons in the air. This emphasizes the connection between *ch'i* and feng shui. To continue:

As the Universal Force or Eternal Energy, it is at the center of Taoist breathing exercises, which also involve the art of smelling and the use of incense. In occult diagrams it is the reason for the preference for asymmetrical design. The *Pao-p'u tzu* states: "Man exists in *ch'i*, and *ch'i* is within man himself. From Heaven and Earth to all kinds of creation, there is nothing which would not require *ch'i* to stay alive. The man who knows how to circulate his *ch'i* maintains his own person and also banishes evils that might harm him."

This sentence refers to the inner cultivation of Taoist sexual alchemy.

The same source mentions a method of casting spells by simply rendering breath (*ch'i*) more abundant. The Taoist Chao Ping used to charm streams by breath so that the water-level dropped as much as twenty feet. Using the same technique, he would light a cooking-fire on thatched roofs without setting light to the dwelling, render boiling water harmless for scalding and prevent dogs from barking.

I have seen these breathing techniques used to form or disperse mists in hollows, particularly those identified as a potential *hsueh*, and to cause water in natural ponds to appear to seethe, while remaining cold. This is the magical application of *ch'i* that, along with a knowledge of certain spirit registers, is at the base of all Taoist magic. Some details of this can also be found in John Blofeld's *The Secret and the Sublime* and Michael Saso's *Taoist Master Chuang.*

As *ch'i* pervades both Heaven and Earth, the *ch'i* are divided into:

1. **Earth *ch'i*** (*ti ch'i*) or host *ch'i,* which have their life in the dragon veins of the earth. These run through the earth and along its watercourses and are subject to decay. They are governed by the Later Heaven Sequence of the trigrams.

2. **Heaven *ch'i*** (*t'ien ch'i*) or guest *ch'i* are affected by the state of *t'ien* and may overrule the effect of Earth *ch'i.* These are governed by the Former Heaven Sequence of trigrams.

The different governance of these two different forms of *ch'i* by the Former Heaven Sequence and the Later Heaven Sequence lies at the root of practical feng shui techniques for using these apparently conflicting *pa kua* sequences.

3. **Weather *ch'i*,** of which there are five, mediate between Earth and Heaven *ch'i* much in the same way that man is midway between Heaven and Earth and has some small say in influencing both. The five weather *ch'i* are rain, fine weather (or sunshine), heat, cold, and wind. Significantly these weather *ch'i,* including wind or *feng* and rain or *shui,* are the moveable *ch'i,* the fluctuating elements distributed between the more fixed *ch'i* of Heaven and Earth. Thus the ability of a feng shui master to judge or control the *ch'i* of Heaven and Earth is admirably reflected in the presence of *feng* and *shui* among the intermediary weather *ch'i.* Not only do the weather *ch'i* mediate between Heaven and Earth *ch'i,* but they partake of the nature of both. They are subject to decay like the Earth *ch'i* and are governed by both sequences of trigrams. Their decay is governed by the fluctuations of *ch'i* that is usually described as "the advancing and the reverting breath."

The cyclical flux and growth cycle of *ch'i* is described by a series called the twelve Palaces, which describe the rise and wane of *ch'i* energy in a human life cycle, but is equally well applicable to the waxing and waning of the *ch'i* of a site (see Table 2).

Table 2. The twelve Palaces (or Life and Growth stages) 十二宮

生	*Sheng*	growth, or to be born
沐浴	*Mu yu*	to be cleansed
冠帶	*Kuan tai*	to come of age (literally to assume cap and girdle)
臨官	*Lin kuan*	to approach officialdom (become an official)
旺 *or* 帝	*Ti wang*	prosperity
衰	*Shuai*	to decay (become weak)
病	*Ping*	to become sick, sickness
死	*Ssu*	to die, death
葬	*Tsang*	to be buried, burial
絕	*Chueh*	conception or soul incarnates
胎	*T'ai*	womb
養	*Yang*	nourishment

Just like the tides of the sea, it is as necessary to receive the influx of life on the incoming tide as it is to lose the waste and detritus on the outgoing tide. This is why the dragon and tiger must be balanced, with the incoming tide of the dragon in the ascendant so that the positive virtues of *ch'i* gradually accumulate rather than being washed away (which would be the case if the yin tiger negative cycle predominated).

The two breaths of nature are, however, essentially one breath. The male and female principles, uniting, constitute the beginning of things; when they disperse, they cause decay, dissolution, and death.

When the breath of *ch'i* is exhausted in the human body, it dies. When it is abundant, feats of almost superhuman strength and skill can be performed. It is obviously very important for one's living space to be supplied with an adequate accumulation of *ch'i*. The adept of internal Chinese alchemy or the martial arts has learned to accumulate *ch'i* in his own body by a hard and exhausting regimen, but for most of us the degree of passive absorption of *ch'i* from our surroundings, be they home or work, is the factor governing our energy and lucidity level. An increase of *ch'i* in a site automatically benefits those living there, and feng shui provides a method of doing this.

The image is clear: the greatest generation of *ch'i* occurs at the point where the lines of the dragon and the tiger are locked together in intercourse. The sexual nature of the spot where there is some "sudden transition from male to female" is the link between *ch'i* as applied to the body of the Earth and *ch'i* as applied to the body of man: in each case it is the same force that is generated by sexual intercourse.

Ch'i interpreted as generated energy explains why the siting of graves is important for the continued fecundity of the descendants of the occupant of the grave, whose families should multiply vigorously if the feng shui of the grave is well judged.

Now as there is only one point of sexual contact between two ranges of hills coupling in the form of tiger and dragon, it is obvious that the supply of prime feng shui sites is extremely limited, especially as owners of such sites were careful to prevent the occurrence of any other burial or building nearby that might draw off the valuable *ch'i*. Other sites on these two ranges of hills are purely tributary *ch'i* sites, just as the various meridians of the body carry a flow of *ch'i* but none so strong as the *haru*, or the genitals themselves.

The Taoist practitioners of sexual yoga and internal alchemy called their art the yoga of the azure dragon and white tiger. The parallel is quite explicit, and not merely symbolical.

How do we interpret the mating of these two symbolic animals? To understand this, it is necessary to consider the nature of the dragon. The Chinese dragon may be understood in many senses: the animal of the eastern quarter, or in the feng shui sense, the writhings of the landscape and the form of mountain ridges. The ridges and lines in the landscape form the body, veins (*lung mei*), and pulse of the dragon while the watercourses and pools and underground watercourses form the dragon's blood. The veins and the water-courses both carry the *ch'i*, the life force of the Earth. Of course, lines of trees, roads, and even railways carry or disperse *ch'i* across the landscape. The geometry of the flow of *ch'i* can be amazingly complex, forming a lattice or a network between the main dragon veins, for no part of the earth is completely dead. Some parts are barren and some are stagnant, but none are totally dead.

The amount of *ch'i* flowing, and whether it accumulates or is rapidly dispersed at any particular point, is the crux of feng shui. An auspicious site or *hsueh* (dragon's lair) needs to be near a good strong flow of *ch'i*, but not necessarily on the main vein or artery, which may even carry away its beneficent influences almost as fast as it brings them! A splitting into many and branching streams of *ch'i* is also a disadvantage, just as the sheet drainage of water can do as much damage to the surface of the earth as a raging channel torrent. Oddly the parallels between an agriculturally desirable drainage system and the most effective flow of *ch'i* are remarkably consistent. The two critical elements of the landscape from a feng shui, and an agricultural, point of view are the mountains (*shan*, 山) and watercourses (*shui*, 水). All else, be it sedimentary plains or steep gorges, is formed by their interaction. As Feuchtwang neatly puts it, "*shan* and *shui* are merely positive and negative of the same thing; the *shan* follow the same lines as *shui* since every *shan* is the back of a *shui*—taking *shui* in its broadest sense . . . whether dry or with water running in it."

Just as the Chinese approach to geography meshes with the more mystical feng shui, so their approach to meteorology invokes the aid of the weather *ch'i* in explaining the seasons. The weather *ch'i* produce, under the combined influence of the five planets and the five Elements, the twenty-four mini-seasons, which are called the "twenty-four breaths of nature." For example, *ch'i* allied to the Element Wood, and guided by Jupiter, produces rain (*shui*); combined with the Element Metal and ruled by Venus, the *ch'i* produces fine weather; joining the Element Fire and influenced by Mars, the *ch'i* produces heat; supported by the Element Water and ruled by Mercury, the *ch'i* produces cold; and with the help of the Element Earth and influenced by Saturn, it causes wind (*feng*).

So goes the theory of Chinese meteorology, which sees the state of the season as an index of the current relationship between Heaven and Earth or Man. Any climatic prodigies therefore will indicate a breakdown in the smooth functioning of this relationship, rather like Shakespeare's use of climatic disturbances in *Macbeth* to indicate the world's outrage at the murder of a king.

How then does this impinge on feng shui? The trained feng shui *hsien-sheng* will note carefully the response of the weather *ch'i* to his client's arrival at the selected site to see if the two are compatible. Further, the feng shui *hsien-sheng* will try and determine a priori the best season for this client to take up residence, so that the then ruling weather *ch'i* will be in full accord with both the main features of the site and of the *pa tzu* (*Ba Zi*) horoscope of its prospective occupier.

When this delay is applied to the burial of the dead, it has not been uncommon for the bones of an immediate relative to remain unburied for some considerable time awaiting an auspicious season. In fact in Amoy [Xiamen] during the nineteenth century, missionaries used to refer rather disrespectfully to the jars of bones that dotted the hillsides awaiting a more propitious disposal as "potted Chinamen." This practice, although actively discouraged, has persisted in some communities to this day, especially among those families who feel they must also save up for an appropriate burial.

But to return to the question at hand: how may we determine the exact location of the flows of *ch'i* and whether any particular dragon vein is favorable or unfavorable, fast-flowing or slow-eddying, and whether tapping a particular spot will result in an accumulation of the precious *ch'i*?

First it is useful to know that where there is a true dragon, there will also be a tiger, and the two will be traceable in the outlines of mountains or hills running in a curved course. Moreover, the dragon's trunk and limbs will often be discernible;

even the very veins and arteries of his body running off from the dragon's heart will appear in the form of ridges or chains of hills.

As a rule, there will be one main accumulation of *ch'i* near the dragon's genitals, while near the extremities of his body the *ch'i* is likely to be milder or even exhausted. At a distance of twenty *li* (six miles) the breath becomes feeble and ineffective. But even near the dragon's heart, the *ch'i*, unless well kept together by surrounding hills and mountains, will be scattered. Where the frontage of any given spot, though enjoying an abundance of *ch'i*, is broad and open on all sides, admitting the wind from all the four quarters, there the *ch'i* will be of no advantage, for the wind will scatter it before it can do any good.

The essence of good feng shui is to trap the *ch'i* energy flowing through the site and accumulate it without allowing it to go stagnant.

One of the classics of feng shui by Kuo P'o says that "*ch'i* rides the winds and disperses," so that windy sites unprotected will lose any accumulated *ch'i*. However, when bounded by water, the *ch'i* halts. Here are the two elements of feng shui, wind and water. The wind if tamed to a gentle breeze will bring the circulating *ch'i*; the water if curved and appropriately oriented will keep the *ch'i* in the site thereby increasing its physical and spiritual fertility. The third main consideration is not to allow the *ch'i* to go torpid or stagnant, in which case it becomes *ssu ch'i*.

If these three things can be achieved by the natural configurations of the landform, then the makings of an excellent lair (*hsueh*, 穴) have been discovered. If this lair has the appropriate balance of yin and yang landforms, then the necessary energy exists to attract the *ch'i*.

The site is referred to as a lair because the selection of dwelling site or house is as essential to man's well-being as the selection of a lair is to an animal. While the animal instinctively selects his dwelling place, man has lost these instincts and needs some guidance to choose the right spot, guidance such as that provided by feng shui.

An ideal site, therefore, is one protected from high winds by a northern screen of hills or trees, a place in which streams and rivers meander slowly, and that nestles in the embrace of hills rather like an armchair, with a view preferably to the south. The horseshoe shape which is repeated many thousands of times in Chinese cemeteries is an artificial representation of the ideal protecting ranges to the rear of the site. The Ming tombs northwest of Peking [Beijing] reflect such an ideal configuration in a natural landform that was obviously selected for that purpose. The lair is usually the nucleus of a more complex system of dragons (*lung*) which extends outward from the lair.

Although there are a number of favorable sites in any dragon configuration, only one will be the perfect site, which is where it is considered that the white tiger of the west and the azure dragon of the east interlock sexually. In any given landscape a number of possible points can be located for this, but according to tradition only one of these, which will be infinitely superior to the others, will be the true point of sexual union. To live in such a site (or perhaps to bury one's ancestors there) guarantees a life rich in spiritual and physical benefits: a site paralleled by the image of the pearl being chased by the dragon (see Figure 4).

However, feng shui, pragmatic as ever, acknowledges that most of us lay our heads in less exalted lairs and consequently provides numerous rules for improving upon their *ch'i* collecting and retaining properties.

The forms and configurations should be looked upon as the body of the dragon; the water and underground springs, the blood and veins of the dragon; the surface of the earth, the skin of the dragon; the foliage upon it, the hair; and the dwellings as the clothes, according to the *Huang-ti Chai-ching,* or "Yellow Emperor's Dwelling Classic." Along the lines of the ridges, both blown by the wind and carried by the water, as well as through the underground channels, flows the vital *ch'i* that feeds the life on the surface of the earth. The direction from which this *ch'i* flows colors it with different qualities— some of them conflicting, some of them complementary. To determine the resultant mix of these *ch'i* flows, the site is often looked upon as a disc or compass card with flows of *ch'i* entering or leaving from various directions.

One school of thought particularly lays stress upon the exact degrees of entry and exit in relation to the center. Obviously if you move some distance from the site under consideration, your new location will stand in a different relationship to the flows of *ch'i* that now enter at a different angle. This Compass approach differs from, but is complementary to, the Form School approach which relies more on the assessment made by the practitioner of the landscape forms of the dragon.

Sha

Although the site should not be windy or exposed as this will result in the dispersal of *ch'i*, the site can also be disadvantageous if it is completely hemmed in so that the air does not circulate, or the water nearby is sluggish and stagnant, or the ground literally gives off damp and stinking exhalations (*sha*), rendering the place unfit either for living inhabitants (for very obvious reasons), or for the burying of the dead (as the corpse would not last long under such damp conditions).

The preservation of the coffin and the bones in the grave was considered very important. It was even asserted that grave sites with a large accumulation of *ch'i*, with the bones of the ancestor well preserved, not only reflect benefit on his descendants but also sometimes actually radiate a luminous glow up through the earth, which is supposed to be visible on occasion. Hence very practical considerations of the right type of soil, absence of insects, and a good drainage system have become part of the rules of feng shui.

Detailed specifications of the type of soil are given by De Groot (1897:953):

> hollow, flat or straight-lined formations do not respire, and are therefore of little or no use for burying or building pur-

poses. In making graves, attention should also be paid to the fact that hard, rocky soil is breathless; compact, reddish loam on the contrary is full of breath and life and consequently prevents a quick decay of the coffin and the corpse, rendering the bones hard, white, and suitable for binding the soul for a long time to the grave. Besides, white ants and other voracious insects are not harboured in such loamy soil, which fact geomancers ascribe to the influence of *ch'i.*

It is interesting to note the element of compulsion in the binding of the soul to the grave, as a necessary prerequisite for good feng shui for the descendants of the soul so bound.

If watercourses near the place run off straight and rapidly, there the *ch'i* is also scattered and wasted before it can serve any beneficial purpose. Only in places where the *ch'i* is "well kept together, being shut in to the right and left, and having a drainage carrying off the water in a winding tortuous course," are the best indications for accumulating *ch'i.*

Taking together all these factors so far outlined we have formed a picture of the conditions necessary for locating the best spot for the accumulation of *ch'i* known to the feng shui *hsien-sheng* as the "dragon's lair." This useful term designates either the tentative site under consideration, or more accurately, a site whose properties have been determined and that satisfactorily accumulates the *ch'i.*

Sha (煞) is the antithesis of *ch'i* and can be translated as "noxious vapor." It is a form of evil *ch'i* and is often called *sha ch'i,* or *feng sha* (noxious wind).

Sha can be produced by a configuration of the landform that leads to the loss of good *ch'i* or actively promotes evil *ch'i,* or it can be generated by conflicting influences and conjunctions as determined by the compass. It can also literally refer to a cold wind issuing from the earth (marked by hollows) or through gaps in the protecting mountain ranges to disturb the accumulation of *ch'i* and render the site inauspicious.

"Secret arrows" are straight lines which by virtue of their power to conduct *ch'i* pierce any accumulations of *ch'i* and reduce its efficacy. These lines can be straight ridges, house-tops, railway embankments, telegraph wires, or any set of parallel straight lines aimed at the spot that is subject to the evil influence of these "secret arrows." These are a specific form of *sha*. Such "secret arrows" can be blocked off from a site by a wall, row of trees, embankment, or octagonal "target boards" with the appropriate deflecting characters written thereon.

As a general rule, which is reflected in the intricacies of Chinese art, the meandering, undulating line conducts *ch'i* while the straight line, sharp bend, or fast watercourse indicates *sha*. In some ways such organic lines are as typical of Chinese civilization as rectangular Cartesian lines are the hallmark of Western civilization. Basic to the nature of feng shui dragon lines and Chinese civilization generally is the curve as opposed to the straight line that expresses itself not only in Western architecture, but also in the ley lines, which it has often been suggested, incorrectly, are the European equivalent of dragon lines. They are in fact diametrically opposed. Straight lines, as we have seen, are anathema in feng shui for they generate *sha* and "secret arrows."

The configuration of many Chinese towns and villages owes its evolution more to the avoidance of *sha* than to the European obsession with the "shortest distance between two points." The larger cities such as Canton [Guangzhou] and Peking [Beijing], although featuring square-gridded streets, are adequately protected as a whole by their correctly aligned city walls and compensatory statues and pagodas.

As a general rule, as straight lines of ridges or chains of hills produce malign influences, so do straight creeks, canals, or rivers. As water is looked upon as the embodiment of wealth and affluence, where water runs off in a straight course it causes the property of those dwelling there to also run off and dissipate like water. Tortuous, curved flow is the indication of the possibility of a beneficial *ch'i* accumulation.

It is interesting that there are also definite geographical advantages to a site found to be in accordance with the rules of feng shui. For example, quite often straight (arrow-like), fast-flowing rivers are located along fault lines. Sharp bends, which are also inauspicious, often indicate underlying structural defects and irregularities. Heavily meandering rivers, however, are likely to be found where there are large deposits of fertile alluvial sediment: good land to settle. Similar parallels in fact give a substantial commonsense background to the dragon-lore of feng shui.

Although some sites may look auspicious by all the rules of feng shui so far outlined, the possibility of noxious exhalations, *sha* or "secret arrows" should always be looked into. Essentially, *sha* is the poisonous opposite of *ch'i*. Continuous straight lines are generally considered to be an evil indication. A typical example might be a line formed by rooftops of the same height pointing in the same direction. Any Western city will provide innumerable examples of this sort of line. Likewise a scarp face rising up in a bold straight line is conducive to the production of *sha*.

Fortunately, in general the existence of *sha*, or a pernicious breath, will betray itself by outward indications. It is said that whenever there is a hill or mountain rising abruptly up from the ground, running in a straight line, or showing an exceedingly rugged appearance unmitigated by any gradual sloping or yin influence, then one can expect to find dangerous breath there. Generally speaking, all straight lines are evil indications, but most especially when a straight line points directly toward the spot where a *hsueh* has been chosen.

Even suppose a place has been found where both the dragon and the tiger are united, each curved like a bow, but with the side ridges running in straight lines (resembling an arrow laid on the bow), then that would be an absolutely dangerous configuration, all the more so for the apparent perfection of the site.

The symbolic arrow will puncture and wound the dragon vein, thereby leaving it to fester and produce *sha*; a fanciful interpretation perhaps, but one taken very seriously by all feng shui *hsien-sheng*, particularly the exponents of the Form School for whom the visible manifestations of the landscape are paramount.

Not only the direct arrow line was to be feared, but also the straight street or railway line that, if directed across the frontage of a site, will effectively drain it very rapidly of its accumulated *ch'i*.

It is in fact this aversion to *sha* that caused in colonial days in China the purchase and subsequent destruction by a Chinese syndicate of one particular piece of railway track that ran straight toward a city whose livelihood it was assumed to be damaging. Straight railway embankments and similar works were looked upon with much disfavor in China.

Straight waterways, a formation that is very uncommon in nature anyway, are also avoided, especially as water is such a good conductor of *ch'i*. Water is symbolic of wealth and a straight stretch of it leading from a site will, according to feng shui, promote the rapid loss of its wealth.

Another curious feng shui contraindication is the presence of free-standing rocks or boulders. If they are integrated with the landscape by being well screened by trees, shrubs, and moss, then their discordant note is muted, but should they be exposed and uncovered, especially if jagged or ugly, they will destroy the flow of beneficent *ch'i* and make for an ill-aspected site.

There are many tales of tombs located in such a neighborhood whose influence continued to be beneficent until accident, climate, or the deliberate act of a malicious enemy uncovered the boulders or felled the trees, resulting immediately in a sudden misfortune, loss of wealth, or disgrace falling upon the descendants and their families. Such accounts have done a great deal to reinforce belief in feng shui.

Hong Kong, where many of the mainland Chinese feng shui *hsien-sheng* retired after the Revolution, is endowed with an abundance of free-standing rocks and boulders scattered about the hillside of the main island, causing it to abound with *sha*. The associated phenomena of loosely held soil slopes has resulted in a systematic tree-planting effort by the government, which is accordingly credited with considerable forethought in the matter of feng shui, as trees are supposed to help mitigate this particular noxious breath.

The early design of Government House, with its curved and sweeping drive, good aspect, and backing by a cordon of trees, has done little to disabuse the populace of their suspicion that the colony's engineer and chief architect was in fact a master feng shui *hsien-sheng.* Since then, the building of the cleaver-shaped Bank of China building, reputedly aimed at this building, has in the opinion of the local feng shui men considerably reduced the auspiciousness of Government House. More recently the chief executive of Hong Kong from China takeover to 2005, Tung Chee-hwa, refused to live here, reputedly because of this diminished feng shui auspiciousness.

Anecdotes about the early feng shui clashes between government and missionaries on the one hand and the populace on the other abound, but perhaps one of the most interesting (it being a sort of negative feng shui) is related by Eitel (1873:53).

> The most malicious influence under which Hong Kong suffers is caused by that curious rock on the edge of the hill near Wanchai [the bar and red light district of Hong Kong island] . . . The Chinese take the rock to represent a female figure which they call the bad woman, and they firmly and seriously believe that all the immorality of Hong Kong, all the recklessness and vice of Taip'ingshan are caused by that wicked rock. So firm is this belief impressed upon the lower classes of Hong Kong that those who profit from immoral practices actually go and worship that rock, spreading out offerings and burning frankincense at its foot. None dare to injure it, and I have been told by many otherwise sensible people that several stonecutters who attempted to quarry at the base of that rock died a sudden death immediately after the attempt.

Just as the authorities could modify the influence of the rock near Wanchai by systematically planting a tree screen around it, so, for a price, an inventive feng shui *hsien-sheng* can allay or modify the worst effects of *sha* or "secret arrows."

The standard method in the latter case is to build a feng shui wall or screen to cut off the sight of the offending quarter: technically out of sight really does mean out of mind, and out of action, in a feng shui context. If the client doesn't wish to spend that kind of money, then the installation of a feng shui mirror surrounded by the eight trigrams in the Former Heaven Sequence could be expected to deflect some of the trouble. Such mirrors are still a common sight in today's Hong Kong, although less common than they used to be in Singapore. More naturally, the planting of trees or the construction of a *ming t'ang* (明堂) pond or tank constantly supplied with fresh water might do the trick, as well as aesthetically improving the environment.

Many villages, hamlets, or individual houses in southeastern China planted their own tree screens or bamboo groves at the rear of the house, with a miniature *ming t'ang* pond in front for this very reason. In fact where the land is flat, trees are often substituted for the traditional protective mountain range. This practice is reinforced by similar suggestions in feng shui books, such as the "Yang Dwelling Classic," which proscribed the planting of trees in front of the house, where the assumed south-facing view was not to be disturbed. Trees were also avidly planted to obscure any free-standing rocks or inauspicious hillocks.

Such trees must be allowed to grow naturally following their own inclinations, without any pruning, cutting, or binding. They should be prolific growers and preferably evergreen (to indicate abundant and continual prosperity). It is an odd coincidence that as the yew fits this description, it has come to be a graveyard guardian in both Europe and China.

Like feng shui walls put up purely to break an inauspicious line of sight, there are groves of specifically designated feng shui trees which are carefully protected from any indiscriminate wood-gathering.

The tree and pond are in many ways the most natural elements of urban or semi-urban feng shui practice, both relying on the munificence of the water dragons for their survival. Pine, symbolic of longevity, is often picked out for service as a single feng shui tree, when it is accorded the respect and offerings usually reserved for a *spiritus loci*, so that its feng shui function may be allied with a type of tree worship.

There is therefore much scope for increasing the beneficent *ch'i* accumulating abilities of the landscape. It is in fact this premise that led to the creation of the exquisite Zen gardens located around many shrines in China and Japan even today. The manipulation of the existing elements of the landscape into these gardens, where nature is enhanced not uprooted, is a specialized application of feng shui. A feng shui practitioner can advise on the location of a new wall in the garden, the position of a statue, or the erection of a screen or tablet to ward off the malicious influences of "secret arrows."

3
Dragon Veins: Form School

Clouds emanate from dragons.

—*I Ching*

It is said by the sages of China that neither Heaven nor Earth is complete in itself, and it is left to Man, the mediator between the two, to complete things and bring them to perfection. The Taoist view is that conscious effort (illumined by a knowledge of the workings of Heaven and Earth) may, among other things, correct the natural outlines of the Earth's surface to a more perfect configuration that will conserve and accumulate *ch'i* to the mutual benefit of the Earth, Man, and in the long term, Heaven. The influence of weather *ch'i* and the cycles of the five Elements is important, but "blind" when compared with the ability of Man to utilize to the fullest extent the latent *ch'i* of his abode, while living, for his own benefit, and, when dead, for the benefit of his descendants.

It is inherent in this system of thought that although Heaven directs the life of man, and Earth conditions this direction, by the improvement of an unfavorable natural (Earth) configuration, man may partly control his own destiny.

In historical times, those with sufficient power or wealth have made such changes, to their own continuing benefit, as they saw it. Hills not quite high enough have been raised; skylines too sharp have been razed. Natural waterways have been diverted to form moats horseshoe in shape, many of which still show up in ordnance survey maps of China or the New Territories of Hong Kong. Straight rivers can be curved or diverted if thought to be dangerous to existing structures.

Quarrying can be stopped if it threatens lines of sight, or the bones or veins of an established dragon, legally if necessary.

Given the necessary resources mountains redolent of the fiery and dangerous potency of Mars can be converted into the squarer outlines of Jupiter, while visually boring flat plateaus sometimes have mounds raised upon them to add an element of yang to an all-yin environment.

The exaggerated style of Chinese landscape artistry will often highlight these features in a manner that is almost unconsciously pedagogic. To analyze a landscape, the feng shui *hsien-sheng* observes a number of generalized location rules qualified by interpretations of particular landforms found in the area under consideration. To determine the location of the dragon's lair the feng shui *hsien-sheng* first walks the length of the ridges above the site to be checked, or in the recent past would have been carried by his servants in a sedan chair, looking for the headwaters of any creek or rill that might indicate the downward flow of the *ch'i* toward a potential lair, or *hsueh*.

Having dismounted from his sedan chair or located such a point he will often, waiting for the instant of inspiration, launch himself down the slope as fast as he can run, taking no conscious heed of the incline as he plummets precipitously toward the base of the hill. If this career is checked by a hollow the other side of which is sufficient to prevent him from continuing his descent, he will mark the spot and return to the top of the ridge. Here he will select the second rill, or breaking-off point of the *ch'i* from the back of the dragon, and, following the same procedure, descend as rapidly as his legs will carry him but without prior direction, descending at the same pace until his headlong flight is checked by yet another rise or hollow.

This too he will mark, and having made several such descents, it is hoped that he will arrive at a common point of intersection. This he will take as the initial potential lair and formally set up the compass here to observe the surrounding landform features. He orients its needle so it matches the red north-south line in the base of the needle well.

Figure 3. Using the feng shui compass in the Ch'ing Dynasty

He assumes that, having been checked in flight (he being a "dragon man"), the *ch'i* will also be checked, pooled, and maybe assimilated at this point. His rapid passage down the hillside also has the second happy result of stimulating any such flow of *ch'i*, although if one looks at the landscape with the cold eye of a geographer, one might notice that quite often animal tracks form what are later to become rills and streams, and by clearing the vegetation by the constant passage of their feet, will predispose the feng shui *hsien-sheng* to follow and deepen these passages. This technique is part of what has been called "riding the dragon."

The practitioner of feng shui would say perhaps that the animals follow the natural line of *ch'i*, rather than the other way around: nevertheless the end result is the same, that having located the confluence of these, he sets up his compass and proceeds to test whether the "lair" is sound in other respects. It must be a rich vein of *ch'i* that is neither decaying nor moribund.

At this point it is necessary for him to ascertain the exact bearings of each of the major forms in the landscape up to the immediately visible horizon, picking initially the major features such as mountaintops, ridges, bends, and streams (that is, those that are visible from the site). As a general rule those streams that are not visible do not affect the site, although the feng shui *hsien-sheng* may in fact check these out to discover the exact direction in which the stream enters or leaves the visible arena.

The sectors of the compass that apply to the main features are then checked, not only for individual auspiciousness, but for compatibility with the site: what influences will they bring. If the initial readings prove favorable, then the detailed delineation of the minor aspects, their relationship to the various members of the family employing the feng shui *hsien-sheng* and to the time of year at which it is proposed to build or bury, are further investigated. However, if there should appear to be a major conflict, then either the family will be notified that a secondary site has been discovered or the entire procedure will be repeated to determine the location of another potential *hsueh*.

Thereafter if the site has been found to be satisfactory, the *hsien-sheng* will visit it at various times of the day to determine how the shadows impinge upon one another, even going to the extent of lighting candles or lanterns on outlying spurs to emphasize the shape of their profile, which may not be immediately obvious in full daylight. Each of these shapes will be taken into account according to the complex rules of the Form School in a balanced decision made on the basis of the number of minor adverse points and their interaction with the major favorable indications of the site.

A report put before the employers of the *hsien-sheng* quite often precipitates the internal family bickering for which feng shui site selection is infamous. A firm ruling from the head of the family will decide the fate of this site, or whether the feng shui *hsien-sheng* is paid a further fee to discover a somewhat more favorable site.

Finally the consultation of the night sky and the actual positions of the constellations on the horizon at that time of the year can either be confirmed directly, or by the use of an ephemeris, the ubiquitous *Tung Sing*.

The basic rules of the Form School are elaborated upon at great lengths in the standard texts such as those by Yang Yung Sung. In each case the rules can apply at any level, from the siting of a city to the orientation of a single room, for the same principles are active macrocosmically and microcosmically In summary, the basic rules are:

1. Buildings, be they tombs or towns, should if possible be constructed on sloping, well-drained land. From a practical point of view, this means the avoidance of badly drained and low-lying areas that may be unhealthy or easily flooded.

2. To the north of the town, village, grove, or house, there should be a mountainous shield or screen of trees protecting the site from the malicious influences traditionally emanating from this quarter.

3. The dead should be buried on the south-facing slope of this shield facing the town and the living. Variations on this general direction will be decided on the basis of the occupant's

horoscope and the projected date of burial. It is interesting to note that the Egyptians traditionally buried their dead and built their necropolises to the west of the towns of the living (i.e., in the direction of the sunset), but when constructing pyramids, for astronomical reasons they always planned to have the entrance on the north side, a piece of information that has guided tomb robbers for many thousands of years.

4. The entrance to the town or home should always be to the south and have a clear view of this quarter, from which come beneficent influences. Obviously it is not always practicable to site something due north or south, and the shape of the local landform will, of course, modify this, but these are the basic requirements. Quite often the geographical place names in a region, particularly those of hills or prominences, will give valuable details about their feng shui orientation, and sometimes there are local traditions that can upset the auspicious orientation with as much as a 90 degree variance from the traditional rules.

5. The landscape betrays the presence of *ch'i* in its positive (yang) form as a dragon, and in its negative (yin) form as a tiger. The two different *ch'i* currents in the Earth's crust, the one male (positive), the other female (negative), are favorable and unfavorable. These are allegorically called, respectively, the azure dragon (青龍) and the white tiger (白虎). The azure dragon must always be to the left (east), and the white tiger to the right (west) of any site (facing outward from the site).

The dragon and tiger are sometimes compared with the lower and upper portions of a man's arm: in the bend of the arm the favorable site must be looked for, in the angle formed by dragon and tiger, in the very point where the two *ch'i* currents cross or copulate. They are most happily placed when they form a complete horseshoe, that is to say, where two ridges of hills starting from one point run out to the right and left in a graceful curve, their extremities gently turning inward toward each other. Such a formation of hills or mountains is the sure index of the presence of a true dragon (see Figure 4).

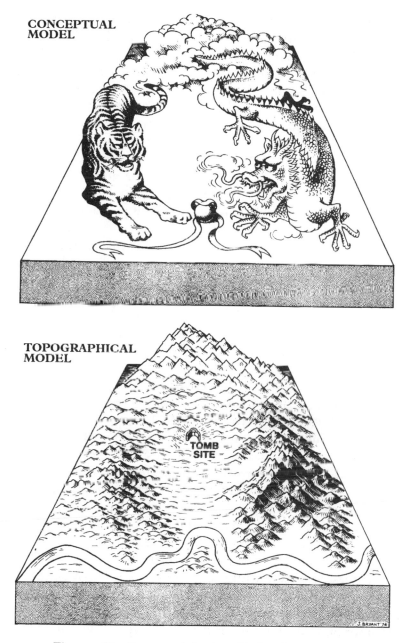

CONCEPTUAL MODEL

TOPOGRAPHICAL MODEL

TOMB SITE

J. BRYANT 74

Figure 4. The dragon and the tiger: ideal and real landscape

A traditional illustration of this is the favorable situation of Canton [Guangzhou], which is placed in the angle formed by two chains of hills running in gentle curves toward where they almost meet each other, forming a complete horseshoe. The chain of hills in the east known as the White Clouds represents the dragon, while the undulating ground on the other side of the river forms the white tiger. The most favorable site in Canton [Guangzhou] may therefore be the ground inside the northern gates, where tiger and dragon are generated. The best side should be hidden "like a modest virgin, loving retirement." It is therefore important to look for a recess where the dragon and tiger may have mated secretly.

In the classic case of the Ming tombs to the northwest of Peking [Beijing], the actual names of the hills and ranges betray their feng shui function, so that the hills to the east of the entrance to the valley of the tombs are actually called "Azure Dragon Hill," while those to the west of the entrance are called the "White Tiger." The last resting place of the ancestors of the emperor, he who incarnates Heaven on Earth, should of course be perfectly located.

6. An extension of the dragon-tiger rule is that if these cannot be perfectly found in the site then the generalized conjunction of "male" and "female" ground will do almost as well. Boldly rising elevations are yang (male), while uneven, softly undulating ground is called yin (or female) ground. On ground where the male characteristics prevail, the best site is on a spot having female characteristics, either visible or indicated by the compass, while on a locality that is on the whole female ground, the spot for a grave or house should have some indications of yang. In each case it should be a spot where there is a transition from male to female, or from female to male ground, and where the surroundings combine both male and female characteristics in the proper proportion—that is male predominating. Where the reverse occurs, the indications are totally against the fortuitous accumulation of *ch'i,* and they will counteract any other favorable configurations.

7. As a consequence of the above, it is apparent that completely flat land is not propitious from a feng shui point of view. In fact, where flat land is used for burial or building, artificial mounds or lines of trees are often incorporated to the north side of the structure, to provide support.

8. If the land proves to be a dragon ridge to the east and a tiger formation to the west, the next point that the feng shui *hsien-sheng* must consider is the proportion of these two elements in the landscape. The ideal proportion delineated by the Taoists is three-fifths male (yang) to two-fifths female (yin), a slightly chauvinistic proportion designed to actively concentrate the benefits of *ch'i* on the site.

In addition to these orientation rules it is necessary to interpret specific landform manifestations.

Shan (山), Mountains

Mountains are the traditional abode of the immortals, of dragons and gods. This is not only because mountains form almost inaccessible retreats, but because they are the symptomatic crust covering the most powerful dragon veins. A flat landscape (just as in some academic Western geographical thinking) is an old, tired, yin worn-down landscape composed of the second-hand silt and detritus washed down from the mountains over the eons. Mountains, however, are the pristine spring of yang forces, the most virile and powerful landscape feature, a fit lair for dragons.

The K'un-Lun range of mountains in the far west of China was often considered to be "the progenitor of all the mountains of the world and the center of the Earth from which the great eastward-flowing rivers of China carry the beneficial influences of the dragon to the coast."

Consequently the form and structure of all the hills visible to the horizon, with special reference to the shape of their summits, is perhaps the most marked mountain indicator of the Form School. It is therefore one of the first requirements of a feng shui *hsien-sheng* that he should be able to tell at a moment's glance which star, planet, and Element is represented by any given mountain (see Table 3). The rules by which each mountain may be referred to one or other of the five planets are very simply defined by Eitel (1873:57):

> If a peak rises up bold and straight, running out into a sharp point, it is identified with Mars and declared to represent the element fire. If the point of a similarly-shaped mountain is broken off and flat but comparatively narrow, it is said to be the embodiment of Jupiter and to represent the element wood. If the top of a mountain forms an extensive plateau, it is the representative of Saturn, and the element earth dwells there. If a mountain runs up high but its peak is softly rounded it is called Venus and represents the element metal. A mountain whose top has the shape of a cupola is looked upon as the representative of Mercury, and the element water rules there.

As a further complication it is necessary to interpret the significance of the cyclical animal of the client's birth date in conjunction with the nature of the prevailing hill form. Thus a person born in a Fire month will be at home with a Fire hill, but a person born in a Wood month would encounter disaster if he built or was buried within sight of such a Fire hill: the symbolic possibility of conflagration is obvious.

Additionally the signification of all the hills or mountains visible from a particular site should be friendly or at least neutral to each other. As with all Chinese philosophical systems, conflict is to be avoided at all cost. Eitel (1873:58) suggests a classic illustration.

> Suppose there is close to a hill resembling Jupiter and therefore representing the element wood, another with the outlines of Mars and corresponding to the element fire, it is manifest that this is a most dangerous conjunction. For instance, the peak of Hong Kong [island], representing the outlines of Jupiter, is under the influence

Table 3. The five Element forms of mountains

Shape	Planet	Element

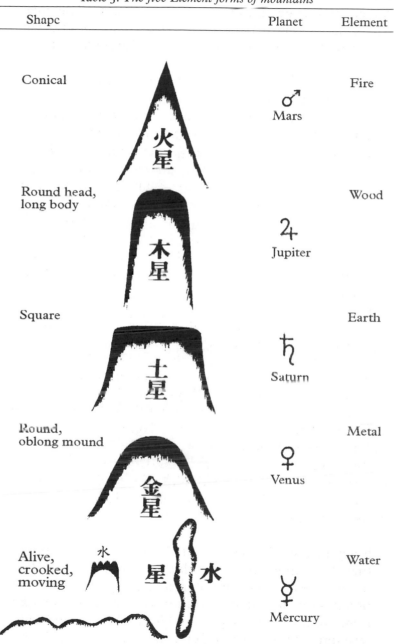

Conical — Mars ♂ — Fire

Round head, long body — Jupiter ♃ — Wood

Square — Saturn ♄ — Earth

Round, oblong mound — Venus ♀ — Metal

Alive, crooked, moving — Mercury ☿ — Water

of wood. Now, at the foot of the peak there is the hill called Taip'ingshan, with the outlines of Mars, and therefore the representative of fire. Now a pile of wood with a fire at the bottom, what is the consequence? Why, it is no wonder that most fires in Hong Kong occur in the Taip'ingshan district.

In addition to the elemental categorization of mountains, there is a separate series of mountain forms that owe their influence on the site they surround to the "nine Flying Stars" or *fei hsing*. The nine Flying Stars are not really "stars" in any usual sense. They are sometimes called "fate-categories," "fate stars," "terrestrial stars," or "atmospheric stars," and are separate from the standard astrological categories which are woven into feng shui practice (see Table 4). Some Chinese translators who have simply consulted a dictionary, and without being at all aware of the nature of the stars under consideration, have mistranslated *fei hsing* as "meteors."

Seven of the nine Flying Stars are identified with the seven stars of the Great Bear or Northern Dipper constellation (*pei-tou,* 北斗) which annually (and daily) rotates around the polestar. As such they correlate with the seasons of the year. The "tail" of the constellation at nightfall points to the quarter attributed to the current season, i.e., in spring to the east, or in autumn to the west.

The nine Flying Stars are also given several compass rings to themselves and are of central importance to the Compass School. One of the best descriptions of these "stars" is to be found in the *Han Lung Ching,* "Classic of the Moving Dragon," by Yang Yun Sung, the patriarch of the Form School of feng shui.

In Form School practice, they are used as categories to define the various hill and mountain shapes. They bear a passing resemblance to the shape of the five elemental forms of mountains, but are much more specific in meaning. For example, the sloping shoulders of the Broken Army (*P'o-chun*) formation would be a disastrous configuration if within sight of the home of a professional soldier, while Military Windings or Career (*Wu-ch'u*) would have the opposite effect.

Literary efforts contributed in the Chinese bureaucratic system to advancement in the civil service. These are enhanced by the presence of the *Wen-ch'u* formation (beneficial for Civil Service or Literary advancement), which might otherwise be interpreted as a Water formation under different circumstances.

There is also a degree of free form interpretation based upon the ability of the feng shui *hsien-sheng* to interpret the yang landforms in relation to the circumstances of the client's family: Eitel (1873:58) again provided classic examples.

> For instance, if a hill resembles in its general contour the form of a broad couch, then its influence will make your sons and grandsons die a premature and violent death. If you build on a mountain which resembles a boat turned bottom upward, your daughters will always be ill, and your sons spend their days in prison.

Eitel also gives an example of the effect of one of the nine Flying Stars:

> If a mountain reminds one in its general outlines of a bell, whilst, at the top there are the outlines of Venus [the *P'o-chun* formation], such a mountain will cause the seven stars of the Great Bear to throw a deadly light upon you which will render you and all the members of your family childless. Most dangerous are also hills that resemble the one or other of the following objects: a basket, a ploughshare, the eye of a horse, a turtle, a terrace, a meadow.

As a general rule the overly yin or rounded mountain is not auspicious.

Table 4. The nine Flying Stars

The seven stars of the Dipper			Meaning	Element	Planet
1	貪狼	T'an-lang	Greedy and Savage (literally "covetous wolf")	Wood	Jupiter
2	巨門	Chu-men	Great Gate or Door	Wood	Jupiter
3	祿存	Lu-ts'un	Rank (salary) Preserved	Earth	Saturn
4	文曲	Wen-ch'u	Civil or Literary Windings (activities)	Water	Mercury
5	廉貞	Lien-chien	Honesty, Purity, and Uprightness	Fire	Mars
6	武曲	Wu-ch'u	Military Windings (activities)	Metal	Venus
7	破軍	P'o-chun	Breaker of the Phalanx Broken Army (breaker of luck)	Metal	Venus

Table 4. The nine Flying Stars

The remaining stars of the Nine						
	Chinese name			Meaning	Element	Planet
8	左輔	Tso-fu		Left assistant of the Celestial Emperor	Earth	Saturn
9	右弼	Yu-pi		Right assistant of the Celestial Emperor	Water	Mercury

向 丁 山 癸

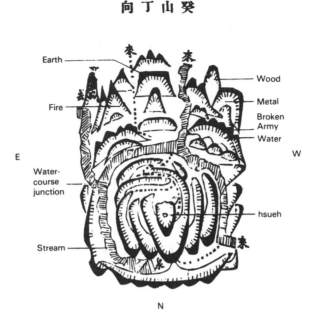

Figure 5. Typical Chinese map of a hsueh

The Chinese caption indicates which of the twenty-four compass directions the *hsueh* aligns with; in this case the site faces *ting* (丁) and "sits" at *kuei* (癸). In other words, it faces the direction marked by a *lo p'an* as between 187.5 and 202.5 degrees, or roughly south (see Table 14 for more details).

A typical site interpreted according to its hill shapes might look something like Figure 5. In this the *hsueh* or "lair" is located in the lower (northern) part of the semi-perspective map and marked as a small circle enfolded by three mountain ranges on either side with an open view to the south (top of the map). Behind the site to the north is the backrest range from which a watercourse progresses to the right. In front of the site (top half of map) there are very obvious mountains of almost every type so far described. Mountains of each of the five Element types are marked, together with one Flying Star mountain (*Po-chun* or Broken Army). When the interrelation of the mountain types has been taken fully into account, the feng shui *hsien-sheng* turns his attention to the watercourses. The hatched areas are watercourses whose exit and entry points to the site are marked by the Chinese character for stream.

Shui, *Water*

In direct opposition to European concepts of orderliness, where a river flowing in a straight line would be a godsend to any engineer or town planner, his Chinese equivalent will earnestly attempt to introduce "natural" curves into a watercourse at the first opportunity. Quite often even when defense is not the objective, a Chinese hydraulic engineer will surround a dwelling or village with a curved moat open on the south side to receive the beneficial *ch'i*. Such diversions of the flow of streams show up in dozens of large-scale ordnance survey maps of areas that have long been Chinese settlements and provide interesting aesthetic relief in the field. For a rice-growing culture, such engineering has never been more than marginally difficult.

An interesting light is thrown on feng shui principles by a description of a perfect site, or dragon's lair, which reads like a sketch of a blind spring. It is logical to postulate that here the dragon is of course in his lair because it is from here the water (i.e., the dragon) emanates before crossing the land as a stream, or being evaporated to form (dragon) clouds.

Apart from their symbolic importance in feng shui, watercourses are the most immediately recognizable feature of any map. They are also easier to interpret than gradients portrayed either by modern contour lines or traditional Chinese semi-perspective drawings.

Watercourses are the most obvious flow lines of *ch'i*. In fact the Chinese homonym of "*ch'i*" means "stream." To interpret the feng shui significance of a watercourse, one must bear in mind the general rule that water flowing fast, or in straight lines, conducts *ch'i* away from a spot rapidly and is therefore undesirable; and that slow, sinuous deep watercourses, on the other hand, are conducive to the accumulation of *ch'i* especially if they form a pool in front of the *hsueh* under consideration.

As a curved and tortuous course is the best indication of the existence of *ch'i* concentrations, so the junction of two watercourses is a key dragon point, sometimes called a *shui ko* (水口) or "water mouth." The feng shui *hsien-sheng* will use a compass to take the precise bearing of this "knot" or junction from the *hsueh*, and it will be a highly significant and easily aligned point.

While the junction should form a graceful curve rather than a union of conflict, the watercourse so established should harmoniously cross and recross the area in front of the site being assessed, thereby bringing a steady flow of benefit without the loss of this resultant upon a rapid and straight egress of the waterway.

Generally stream confluences are beneficial because of the concentration of *ch'i*, while the branching of a stream flowing through coarse sediment or at the delta of a river is dispersive of *ch'i*. Sharp bends, like straight lines, are unfavorable, as they act like "secret arrows" destroying or removing the *ch'i* accumulations. Meanders in the watercourse are much more conductive, as the natural shape of a dragon is that of sinuous meandering.

It is certainly true from a geographical point of view that any watercourse passing through a uniform sediment will automatically meander, so the presence of a straight stream would clearly indicate to both geomancer and geographer an underlying fault in the structure of the land, harmful psychically, as well as revealing at a physical level.

Edkins (1872:75) outlined the rules of stream flow as follows:

the dragon may be traced to its source. It is observable in the flow of the mountain stream, or in the contour of the earth. The hollow river bed, and the variety of hill and valley are caused by the dragon. Trace the water of valley to its source. That is the point from which commences the influence that controls human destiny. Water is the element in which the dragon delights. Its winding shape as it meanders through a plain gives evidence of this, for the dragon prefers crooked paths. Since then the dragon gives prosperity, elevates the king and the sage, and is the symbol of all exaltation, social, political or moral, it is all-important to consider the position of water when selecting the site of the grave.

Edkins further illustrates this with a traditional example:

In the valley of the Ming tombs the water flows from the North-west, passes under a bridge in front of the grave of the Emperor Yung-lo, and then pursues its way down towards the plain of Peking [Beijing] on the south east. Hills in horse shoe form embrace the valley. The feng shui is good.

Apart from the naturalistic observations of the Form School, the practitioners of the Compass School use the precise points of junction, appearance, disappearance and pooling of a watercourse as sighting lines:

The chief use of the geomancer's compass is to determine in regard to the water, the direction of flow, the primary source, the points of junction, and the points from which it starts afresh at a new angle.

The configuration of water to the south is particularly important in assessing the potential of the site for wealth attraction:

Before a tomb must be running water. Riches and rank flow like water capriciously from one point to another. Hence riches and rank are supposed to depend on the undisturbed flow of the stream which passes under the bridge in front of the site . . . Riches and rank are attached to flowing water, and if due care is taken by the geomancer and by the posterity of the dead, a perpetual stream of worldly honour and wealth may be expected to flow into the possession of the family.

Again, perhaps easier than with mountain shapes, the landscape can be altered by man to improve the feng shui. Bends can be put in straight river stretches or sharp bends can be rounded (although these are more likely geographically to occur in rocky country rather than soft sediment, and therefore are more difficult to rectify).

Even artificial confluences or branches can be created. Preferably the dragon liar or *hsueh* should be situated nestled among branches of a river rather than directly on a main or trunk watercourse, especially if the main watercourse runs too fast to accumulate *ch'i*. The more branches, which are the arteries or pulse of the Earth, the more potent the *ch'i* accumulation.

Water, however, is very necessary in one form or another, for a barren site would indicate barren offspring, a fate of the first order of evil to a family- or progeny-oriented society. A lack of branching or joining watercourses is also to a lesser extent looked upon as having this effect, apart from probably indicating a low local rainfall.

A stream flowing from the east or the west is auspicious if it flows directly toward the *hsueh*, deflects around in front of it, and then meanders, for the *ch'i* brought by the stream enters the *hsueh* directly (by a straight stretch of water) but is taken away from the *hsueh* indirectly (by a curved path that is slower): it therefore accumulates.

Of course, if the water is in the south (forming the traditional *ming t'ang* or Heaven Pool), it must be calm and still, and if possible, the stream entering it, and especially the stream leaving it, should be out of sight of the *hsueh*, so that there is no *visible* loss of the *ch'i* accumulated by the pool downhill from the *hsueh*.

The direction in which the water enters and leaves the pool is useful in computing its feng shui value, for the Lo shu diagram of nine squares (with the trigrams) indicates which members of the family are particularly singled out for one fate or another by matching the diagram with the pool's orientation. Details of the relationship of the eight trigrams to the entry and the exit points are to be found in the next chapter (see Table 8).

The *Shui lung ching* or "Water Dragon Classic" (c. seventeenth century AD) is a specialized manual devoted to the formation of water dragons. The dragon referred to in this Form School classic is the energy and coiling of the surface water flow, a "water dragon" reflected in the shape of its watercourses.

It is slightly confusing that the term "dragon" can in a Compass School manual instead refer to a sexagenary character combination (made by combining one of the ten Heavenly Stems with one of the twelve Earthly Branches of the same sex), not a physical feature. For example, the dragons referred to without any qualifications in Wu Wang Kang's *Lo Ching Chieh* or "Explanation of the Compass," and most other manuals, are this sexagenary combination.

The "Water Dragon Classic" classifies watercourses into trunks and branches. The *hsueh* should be located among the latter. Feuchtwang (1974:130) summarizes these doctrines:

> Water is the path of *ch'i* and branches, otherwise called inner *ch'i* "stop" or may be tapped and are productive, whereas trunks or outer *ch'i* merely surround the *hsueh*. The "Water Dragon Classic" contains several diagrams showing different types of watercourse formation, indicating with a dot where the *hsueh* is, and explaining which are lucky and what each formation signifies. Like the shapes of rocks they too may indicate Elements, animals of the Four Quarters, *hsiu* constellations and many other things besides. The *hsiu* [*sic*, should be *hsueh*] must be at the stomach of the dragon, surrounded by it, just as it should nestle protected at the fork of the mountain ridges.

The inner *ch'i*, or stream branches, feed into the outer *ch'i*, or the trunk of the river. The more branches the trunk has, the more potent it will be. According to the "Water Dragon Classic" the trunks are the arteries or pulses of the *Ta Ti*, the Great Earth. As the main pulse flows through the main river trunk, it is wise to site the *hsueh* among the clustered

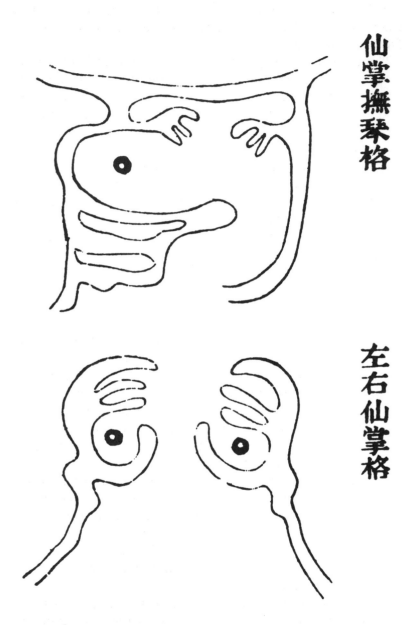

仙掌撫琴格

左右仙掌格

Figure 6. River formations and feng shui sites

branches rather than too close to the trunk or main stream, which runs too fast to allow the gentle penetration of *ch'i* into the house or grave.

The main instrument of landscape sculpture is of course water, or *shui*. This not only carves the mountains and valleys physically but flows through the earth conveying the *ch'i*. From the water that flows on the surface in streams, rivers, and pools, dragons rise into the air, as the water itself evaporates.

Wind, or *feng*, distributes the water vapor as clouds, which, taking the form of dragons in the air, consolidate finally to precipitate life-giving rain on to mountains, the traditional lair of these dragons. The elements wind and water are of course the essence of feng shui, which affects the earth and the life on it.

Feng, Wind

Similar feng shui considerations apply to the flow of that other surface fluid, wind. As the dragons move through the water vapor in the air, their forms are adopted by the clouds. Dragons assume the clouds, or the clouds assume the dragons, as clothes take the shape of the underlying body. Similarly the convoluted windings of the rivers, explainable by no geographer or hydrologist, are the clothes and manifestation of the terrestrial water dragons.

Whether the dragon wears airy apparel or land-locked apparel, it is the same creature, for even as Hermes Trismegistus said, "as above, so below," so it is in Chinese culture where the dragon penetrates both the sky above and the earth below. The form of a dragon is sometimes adopted by the precise curling of a burning joss stick in a draftless room, a million protean dragon limbs.

Not only is traditional Chinese imagery more picturesque, it is also closer to the tenuous life of the forms of air than any physicist might encapsulate in a formula, no matter how abstruse. The belief that dragons lived in streams or oceans but could fly up to clouds only to return again to rivers reveals a systematic knowledge of the connection between evaporation, cloud formation, and rain. It is in fact the wind, *feng*, which carries the dragons of water, *shui*, aloft to form clouds and, from these, rain. The falling of the rain affects the landscape by generating patterns in the course of its return to the sea, via the drainage system of rivers, which carve the shape of the landscape, eroding valleys, leaving mountain ranges, and forming plains. So the very shape of the dragons of earth are conditioned by the "flight and return" of the watery dragons to their home.

What appeared then to be three different "types" of dragons can now be seen to be the three interlocking parts of one continuous natural process. The Chinese vision of this is a vision of the breath of life rather than the mechanical version of the geographer who defines the cycle in terms that he can recreate in a sandpit or a laboratory.

Thus dragons, which must not be confused with the European fire-breathing variety that made St. George a household word, are the animating essence of the natural system that provided the rice-growing farmer with the essentials for cultivation, or the possibility of rapid destruction: truly a beast to be feared.

Dragons are of course not just the animating spirit, but also the very form of the collaboration between *feng* and *shui* to raise aloft those exotic shapes that clouds often take, which drift inland to release their fertilizing rains on the mountaintops, the traditional home of the Dragon Kings who regulate the whole process. Dragon Kings control the weather, just as they mediate between Heaven and Earth, while the five weather *ch'i* ply the space between Heaven and Earth: the lightning, rain, wind, sunshine, and fine weather, conveying the effects of the yang Heaven *ch'i* to the yin Earth *ch'i*.

It is said that if wind has access to a site from all sides, it will scatter the *ch'i* before it has time to accumulate. If, however, the wind is more mellow, then the vital breath of the earth, *ch'i*, is retained. There is quite a striking parallel between the flow of air and the flow of *ch'i*, as wind itself, like water, is considered to be one of the five weather *ch'i* that mediate between Heaven and Earth.

It is strange that of all the books on feng shui, although many mention watercourses (*shui*), there is very little mention of wind (*feng*), except by implication, perhaps because of the impermanent nature of this aspect of the Earth's surface. There are of course references to *hsueh* in hollows protected from strong winds, but not so shielded that the air stagnates. As the dragons of Earth (*ti*) must be reflected in the dragons of Heaven (*t'ien*), and as the wind that blows between them represents Man, feng shui is obviously designed to place Man in the best possible relationship with the dragons of both Heaven and Earth.

Compass Feng Shui—*Li ch'i*

4
Time and Tides: Feng Shui Numbers

If a human ruler likes to destroy eggs and nests, the phoenix will not rise. If he likes to drain the waters and take out all the fishes, the dragon will not come. If he likes to kill pregnant animals and murder their young, the unicorn will not appear. If he likes stopping the watercourses and filling up the valleys, the tortoise will not show itself.

— *Ta Tai Li Chi*

Much of what appears to be intuitive reasoning in feng shui is in fact bounded by the Chinese reverence for law, order, and mathematics. A quick glance at the framework of the laws, or *li*, that govern the Chinese cosmology provides us with a basic vocabulary and background to feng shui terms.

1 Heaven

At the center of the system is the unity often translated as Heaven (*t'ien*) impersonal, all-powerful, and rather distant.

2 Yang and Yin

T'ien breathes, and light (yang) and dark (yin) are created. These are represented in the *I Ching* as the whole line (yang) and broken line (yin). As the whole line is one thing and the broken line is two things, yang is equated to one and yin to two: it follows that all odd numbers are yang and all even numbers are yin. Therefore the mating of odd and even numbered *ch'i* flows is considered a beneficial combination.

As the ancient literal meaning of yin implies "the shady north side of a hill," while yang suggests "the sunny south side of a hill," immediately you have a direct application to the surface of the Earth.

Yin and yang are relative. Yin governs the Earth, all that is negative, female, dark, water, soft, cold, deadly, or still; while yang governs Heaven and all that is positive, male, light, fiery, hard, warm, living, and moving. Of the combination and permutation of the yang and the yin is formed the rest of the universe whose life and breath is *ch'i*.

3 Primes

The term *Three Primes* usually applies to the division of creation into the worlds of Heaven, Man (or Humankind), and Earth. This division is also reflected in the construction of the *lo p'an*, in the three Plates: Earth, Man, and Heaven. It is also reflected in the sequencing of some of the divisions around the rings.

4 Four Seasons

In the first chapter we touched briefly upon the orientation of the four quarters. Obviously summer, being the hottest season, is associated with the south, while spring is to be found in the place of the rising sun, the east. The remaining seasons face their opposites, autumn in the west, and winter in the north.

Additionally if we ascribe the full yang (male) trigram to summer, and the completely yin (female) trigram to winter, we indicate an increase in yin from autumn to winter, and a waxing of yang from spring to summer.

The sun rises in the east, just as the year begins in spring; reaches its peak in the south (midsummer); sets in the west (autumn); and is dark in the north (midwinter). Consequently the seasons are attributed to the four quarters:

Spring—East (equal yang and yin)
Summer—South (maximum yang)
Autumn—West (equal yang and yin)
Winter—North (maximum yin)

Furthermore, the five Elements of the Chinese can be allocated to the seasons and hence to the compass directions, with Fire going to the red phoenix of summer, and Water to the cold north, Wood to east (spring), and Metal to west. The fifth Element, Earth, is the odd one out, being located at the center.

This correlation between feng shui directions and the seasons is often used as a reason to suggest that as the seasons are reversed in the southern hemisphere, so should feng shui directions be reversed. There are a number of variations on this designed to facilitate feng shui practice in the southern hemisphere. However this is missing the point, for the main instrument of feng shui, the compass, still points in the same direction no matter what hemisphere you are in. Furthermore, the sun still rises in the east and sets in the west, wherever you are, China or "down under" in Australia. Consequently as the things that have most effect on *ch'i* flow are the same in both hemispheres, so the practice of feng shui should follow the same rules. In application this is so.

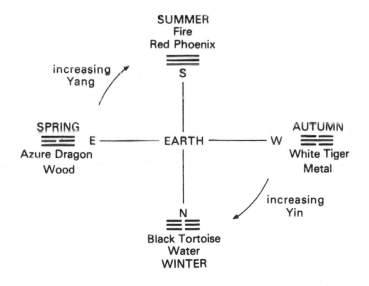

Figure 7. The seasonal waxing and waning of yin and yang

4 Celestial Animals

These four directions are marked by four Celestial Animals, one at each quarter:

> East—the Green/Blue or Azure Dragon
> South—the Red Bird (sometimes translated as vermilion bird, or phoenix)
> West—the White Tiger
> North—the Black Tortoise in intimate embrace with a snake

If you read again the quote at the beginning of this chapter, you will see that these four animals are mentioned, the phoenix (Red Bird), the dragon, the unicorn (instead of the tiger), and the tortoise. The quote is a subtle explanation of the function of these four animals.

A feng shui practitioner will often use these animals as shorthand for directions, saying for example, that a certain building needs support from the black tortoise (the north), or that water helps to strengthen the azure dragon (in the east). There is a further refinement of these four directional animals, and that is that they can also refer to localized directions as determined from the house in question. If you imagine yourself standing in the front doorway of a house and looking outward, then:

> Black Tortoise = behind you (and the house)
> Red Bird = in front of you (and the house)
> Azure Dragon = to your left
> White Tiger = to your right

There is no conflict between these two uses of the four Animals, as long as you don't try to mix them.

5 The Five Elements—*Wu Hsing* (五行)

The five Elements of the Chinese are different from the four ancient Greek Elements of Fire, Air, Earth, and Water inasmuch as they include Wood, which is organic matter and signifies the whole vegetative cover of the Earth, not just trees, and Metal, which symbolizes things fabricated by man or purified from the Earth.

The Elements are:

Water	*shui*	水
Fire	*huo*	火
Wood	*mu*	木
Metal	*chin*	金
Earth	*t'u*	土

Interestingly, air, *feng*, is left out, although water, *shui*, is there. In a way the Chinese elemental view of the Universe is more ecologically oriented than the Greek view. Additionally, the Chinese talk of an order of mutual production and mutual destruction of the Elements while the classical Greek system is more static.

The whole concept of the life and breath, *ch'i*, of the earth is so obvious to a Chinese but so alien to a European. This early worldview generated separately by each of the two cultures has helped reinforce this difference.

It is a little misleading, however, to refer to these five as "Elements," for *hsing* indicates movement, so perhaps "the five moving agents" might be a more appropriate name for the Elements. This certainly reinforces the idea that they generate and destroy each other in a continually moving cycle. Like the trigrams and hexagrams of the "Book of Changes," the *I Ching*, these are also symbols of change and transformation.

The Taoist concept that the Universe is a continually changing panorama of the "myriad things," in which the activity of change and the Great Absolute behind change are the only constants, provides a backdrop for the theory of the "five moving agents."

烏龜背書（洛書）

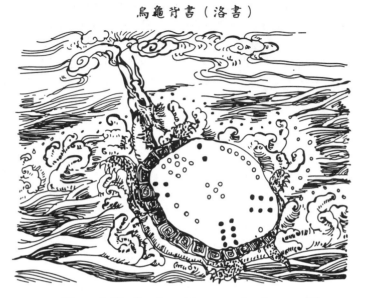

Figure 8. The Lo shu turtle as seen by the great Yu

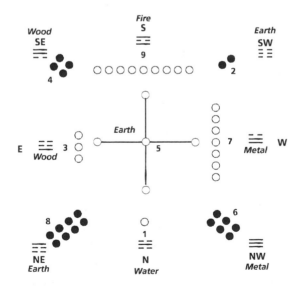

Figure 9. The relationship between the Lo shu,
the eight trigrams, and the compass directions

There are formulas that explain this interaction in terms of the five Elements. Two of the most ancient ones are the Ho t'u and the Lo shu, and these will be examined more closely in connection with the eight trigrams. The first portrays the relationships of the five Elements in the Former Heaven Sequence, in their yang aspect. The Elements give birth to each other in the order shown in Figure 10. Thus, Wood burns to produce Fire, which results in ash (or Earth) in which Metal may be found. Metal is also found in the veins of the earth from which (according to Chinese thought) sprang the underground streams (Water) that nourish vegetation and produce Wood.

The Later Heaven Sequence of the trigrams indicates the destructive order of the Elements. Each Element destroys another in the sequence as shown in Figure 11.

Both these cycles are more easily appreciated in terms of the wide range of things covered by the "Elements." Feuchtwang (1974:42) admirably explains it:

> Wood is understood to be all vegetation, which is fed by Water, and swallows, covers, binds earth, is cut down by metal implements and [which Fire] ignites; if Water is understood to be all forms of fluid including the liquefication of metal by fire, and which can be solidified by being stanched with earth; and if Earth is understood to mean all mixed, impure, and inanimate substances including the ash produced by fire.

When these five Elements are considered in relation to other fields of Chinese thought, a wide-ranging set of correspondences is evolved. These form the background to much traditional Chinese philosophy and conjecture and are also part of the unarticulated fivefold associations taken for granted by a practitioner of feng shui. Some of these correspondences are shown in Table 5.

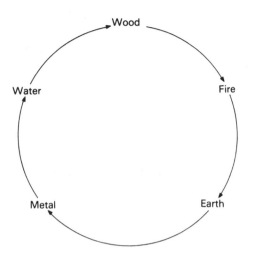

Figure 10. The mutual production order of the Elements

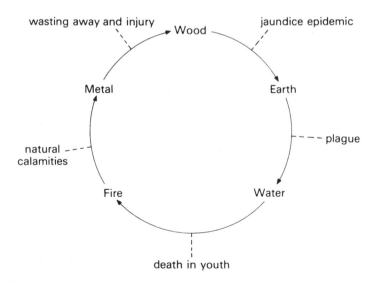

Figure 11. The mutual destruction order of the Elements

Table 5. The five Elements according to the Former Heaven Sequence

	木	火	土	金	水
Element	Wood	Fire	Earth	Metal	Water
Direction	East	South	Center	West	North
Color	Blue/green	Red	Yellow	White	Black
Season	Spring	Summer	—	Autumn	Winter
Heavenly Stems					
(Yin)	8 *i*	2 *ting*	10 *chi*	4 *hsin*	6 *kuei*
(Yang)	3 *chia*	7 *ping*	5 *wu*	9 *keng*	1 *jen*
Climate	Windy	Hot	Humid	Dry	Cold
Mountains	T'ai-shan	Heng-shan (in Hunan)	Sung-shan	Hua-shan (in Hopei)	Heng-shan
Planets	Jupiter	Mars	Saturn	Venus	Mercury
Animals	Azure Dragon	Phoenix/Red Bird	Yellow Snake/Yellow Dragon	White Tiger	Snake and Tortoise/Dark Warrior
Orifices	Eyes	Ears	Mouth	Nose	Anus and Vulva
Emperors	Fu-Hsi	Shen-Nung	Huang-ti	Shao-hao	Chuan-hsu
Qualities	Formable	Burning and ascending	Producing edible vegetation	Malleable and changeable	Soaking and descending
5 Classes of Animal	Scaly (fishes)	Feathered (birds)	Naked (man)	Hairy (mammals)	Shell-covered (invertebrates)
5 Domestic Animals	Sheep	Fowl	Ox	Dog	Pig
Number	8	7	5	9	6
Yin/Yang	lesser yang	greater yang		lesser yin	greater yin
Weather Ch'i	Wind	Heat	Sunshine	Cold	Rain

8 Pa Kua, the Eight Trigrams (八卦) of the I Ching

The I Ching is a binary system of divination derived from the two basic units yin and yang, respectively, the female broken line (– –) and the male unbroken line (—).

A trigram or kua is a three-tier combination of either yin or yang lines: consequently there are 2³ or eight possible trigrams.

Table 6. The eight trigrams or pa kua

Trigram		Meaning	Kua
Ch'ien	乾	Heaven, the sky, the celestial sphere	☰
Tui	兌	Watery exhalations, vapors, clouds	☱
Li	離	Fire, heat, the sun, light, lightning	☲
Chen	震	Thunder	☳
Hsun	巽	Wind and wood	☴
K'an	坎	Water, rivers, lakes, seas, and so on	☵
Ken	艮	Mountains	☶
K'un	坤	Earth, terrestrial matter	☷

The trigrams are combined with one another to form 8 by 8 combinations, that is, 64 hexagrams. The words trigram and hexagram (not to be confused with the Western hexagram or Star of David, which is two interlocking triangles) purely indicate the number of lines in each of these two types of figure. In Chinese both figures are called kua, although sometimes hexagrams are referred to as ta kua or "big kua." It is the hexagram that is the final product of the I Ching divinatory process and that conveys the answer to the question posed.

Each of the hexagrams has a commentary (depending on the configuration of its lines) reputedly written by King Wen and the Duke of Chou in the twelfth century BC, and this forms the bulk of the I Ching text.

Most English translations of the I Ching of necessity place emphasis upon the actual text or the divinatory answers rather than on the intrinsic meaning of the trigrams and hexagrams themselves, which are much more related to Chinese numerical methods of interpretation. These meanings are given in the so-called "wings" or later appendices of the *I Ching* reputedly written by Confucius. These "wings" are much older than the commentaries that often take the majority of the space in current English editions of that great classic. Such phrases in the *I Ching* wings as "K'an is water, the trigram of due north, where the ten thousand things return" are a specific indication of the relation between this trigram and north in the Later Heaven Sequence.

The trigrams are attributed to the points of the compass in two distinct and separate arrangements. These are referred to respectively as the Former Heaven Sequence (allegedly devised by Fu-Hsi and probably the earlier of the two) and the Later Heaven Sequence (identified with King Wen, the first ruler of the Chou [Zhou] Dynasty). Although the history behind these two arrangements need not concern us, the fact that the two arrangements are radically different is important. The two sequences are shown in Figures 12 and 13. Of these, as a general rule, the Later Heaven Sequence is used in practice, while the Former Heaven Sequence is used in theoretical applications.

The lines of the trigrams closest to the center of the circle are the lowest lines and, as with the hexagrams, are counted as the first line. Remember also that the south faces the top of the page, and the north the bottom, in line with Chinese practice and the belief that the south was the most beneficent of the compass points and should therefore be at the top.

Usually, line 1 of the trigram determines the sex of each trigram, the middle line the next criterion of relative yin- or yangness. The third line (i.e., outermost or top) is the least crucial. This way a hierarchy can be built up extending from Ch'ien to K'un, with the yang lower line trigrams preceding the yin lower line trigrams.

The Former Heaven Sequence is the ideal version, while the Later Heaven Sequence is the practical application of the trigrams to the earth. The Former Heaven Sequence is appropriately enough attributable to the Heaven Plate and

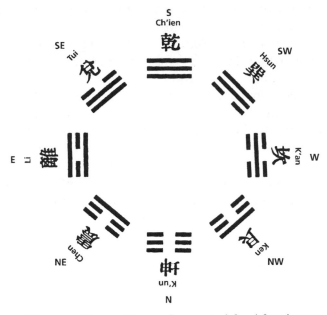

Figure 12. Former Heaven Sequence of the eight trigrams

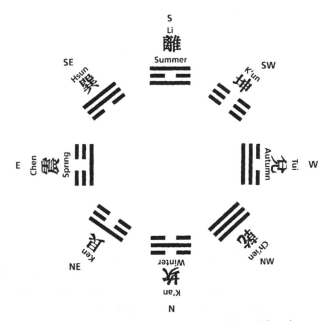

Figure 13. Later Heaven Sequence of the eight trigrams

the Later Heaven Sequence to the Earth Plate on the feng shui compass.

The Former Heaven Sequence corresponds with the Ho t'u diagram while the Later Heaven Sequence corresponds with the Lo shu diagram. Consequently there are more feng shui formulas dependent upon the Lo shu than the Ho t'u. In the Chinese original of the Lo shu there are nine groups of dots representing the numbers 1 to 9 rather than numbers.

The Lo shu is usually shown in the form of a three by three magic square. The numbers in any rank, file, or diagonal of the square always add up to fifteen, which happens to be the number of days in each of the twenty-four phases of the solar year.

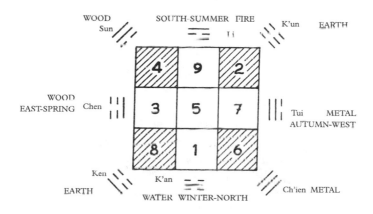

Figure 14. The Lo shu and the eight trigrams

The Later Heaven Sequence of trigrams is generated from the Lo shu as shown in Figure 14. Note that the odd (or yin) numbers form the cardinal points, and the even (or yang) numbers the intercardinal points. These nine chambers can be considered as the nine Palaces or *kong* (宮) of the *Ming T'ang,* the temple through which the Emperor was supposed to circulate according to the season of the year. On a smaller scale they are associated with each of the eight cardinal and intercardinal directions with a trigram, and also provide an ascription of trigrams to each of the rooms of a house or temple built on the traditional square plan, with the central courtyard (square 5) not associated with any specific trigram.

The trigrams thus provide indications of the best rooms of a house for specific purposes or for specific members of the family. As each trigram is associated with one or another member so he is better served if his bedroom is located in this quarter of the house. On a larger scale trigrams help determine the most appropriate direction for doorways or city gates.

When considering a building site, the trigrams are also used to evaluate watercourse entry and exit points. The *Lo Ching Chieh* or "Explanations of the Compass" points out that certain entry and exit points of a watercourse may conflict, if one is judged by the Former Heaven Sequence and the other by the Later Heaven Sequence.

If these points of the compass are attributed to the same trigram (but in different sequences), then the site is considered inauspicious. Thus if the water enters by the compass point of the K'un trigram (in one sequence), and leaves by the K'un direction (according to the other sequence) then the site will not be auspicious. The flow of *ch'i* that connects a trigram with itself, connects the two sequences, and this causes a "short circuit" between Heaven and Earth, thus rendering the site unusable. This in fact is a very important and practical Water Dragon formula.

The Later Heaven Sequence is used for the detection of yin-yang harmony or disharmony at particular points, whereas the Former Heaven Sequence indicates the circular waxing and waning of yin and yang in the archetypal or Heavenly form.

Although the two sequences appear to contradict each other, the logic of the system is preserved if they are considered separately, and if it is remembered that the Former Heaven Sequence stands for the Heavenly order, while the Later Heaven Sequence treats the less perfect cycles of seasons, and manifestations on the Earth itself and is thus prominent in the Earth Plate of the feng shui compass.

It is important to understand the nature of each trigram before progressing any further. For the correspondences of the trigrams see also Table 8, but the essence of each trigram is as follows:

Ch'ien (乾) corresponds to immobility and strength. It represents a horse, the head, the heavenly sphere, a father, a prince, roundness, jade, metal, cold, ice, red colors, and the fruit of trees.

K'un (坤) represents docility, cattle, the belly, Mother Earth, cloth, cauldrons, parsimony, a heifer, large carts, figures, a multitude, a handle, and dark colors.

Chen (震) indicates motion. It represents a dragon, i.e., the animal of the east (in the Later Heaven Sequence). It also indicates the feet, an eldest son, thunder, dark-yellow colors, development, high roads, decision, vehemence, bamboo, and rushes.

Hsun (巽) means penetration, and indicates a fowl, the thighs, an eldest daughter, wood, wind, whiteness, length, height, a backward and forward motion, bald-headedness, and a broad forehead.

Li (離) means beauty and brightness. It represents a pheasant, the bird of the south (in the Later Heaven Sequence), eyes, the middle daughter, the sun, lightning, helmets, spears and swords, a large-bellied man, dryness, turtles, crabs, spiral univalves, mussels, and tortoises.

K'an (坎) signifies peril, a pig, the ears, the middle son, water, channels and streams, hidden things, alternate straightness and crookedness, a bow, a wheel, anxiety, distress of mind, pain in the ears, a blood-red color, high spirits, drooping head, a shambling step; finally thieves and strong trees.

Ken (艮) indicates stoppage, a dog, the hands, a youngest son, paths and roads, small rocks, gates, fruits and cucumbers, porters or eunuchs, finger rings, rats, and birds with large bills.

Tui (兌) means pleasure, a sheep, the mouth, a youngest daughter, mediums, the tongue, a concubine, and so forth.

For feng shui the significance of, for example, the relationship between trigrams and family members is of vital importance when considering which member of a family will receive the most benefit by having his or her representative trigram aligned on the main axis of a site under examination.

The symbolic animals are cardinal point indications for the Later Heaven Sequence, just as are the Element or seasonal attributions.

As various members of the family from elder son through elder daughter top youngest son and youngest daughter all have an attribution to one particular compass point, the son or daughter whose point has a "ceasing *ch'i*" in their quarter at the time of their parents' burial is not going to benefit as much from the feng shui qualities of the burial as his brothers and sisters and will therefore argue for a stay of proceedings or a change of site until their compass point is better aspected. Of course, if it is a big family (that is, one where most compass points are covered by family members), there is never going to be an all-around favorable burial time and place. Sometimes it follows that there looks as though there is never going to be a burial! For attribution of compass points to family members see Table 7.

Table 7. *The members of the family distributed according to the Former Heaven Sequence*

Compass Point	Trigram	Family Member
S	Ch'ien	Father
N	K'un	Mother
SW	Tui	eldest son
E	Li	middle son
NW	Chen	youngest son
NE	Ken	eldest daughter
W	K'an	middle daughter
SE	Hsun	youngest daughter

9 The Flying Stars

The nine Flying Stars or *fei hsing* (飛星) are personifications of the fluctuating tides of *ch'i* that move through the Nine

Table 8. *The trigrams according to the Later Heaven Sequence*

Later Heaven Sequence compass point	Trigram	Family member	Part of the human body	Natural phenomenon	Element	Season
NW	Ch'ien (乾)	Father	Head	Heaven	Metal	Heaven
SW	K'un (坤)	Mother	Belly	Earth	Earth	Earth
E	Chen (震)	Eldest Son	Foot	Thunder	(Wood)	Spring
SE	Hsun (巽)	Eldest daughter	Thighs	Wind	Wood	
N	K'an (坎)	Middle son	Ear	Moon	Water	Winter
S	Li (離)	Middle daughter	Eye	Sun, lightning	Fire	Summer
NE	Ken (艮)	Youngest son	Hand	Mountain	(Wood)	
W	Tui (兑)	Youngest daughter	Mouth	Lake	(Metal)	Autumn

Palaces into which any building can be divided (the eight directions plus the Central Palace).

Table 9. The nine Flying Stars of the Northern Dipper (九星北斗)

"Star"		Name	Name pinyin	Meaning
1	貪狼	T'an lang	tan lang	Hungry Wolf
2	巨門	Chu-men	ju men	Great Gate
3	祿存	Lu-ts'un	lu cun	Salary Preserved
4	文曲	Wen-ch'u	wen qu	Literary Career
5	廉真	Lien-chen	lian zhen	Purity/Uprightness
6	武曲	Wu-ch'u	wu qu	Military Career
7	破軍	P'o-chun	po jun	Breaker of Armies
8	左輔	Tsuo-fu	zuo fu	Left Assistant
9	右弼	Yu-pi	you bi	Right Assistant
	輔弼	Fu-pi	fu bi	Both Assistants*

* The last two are sometimes taken together as one Star.

10 The Ten Heavenly Stems

As their name implies, the ten Heavenly Stems apply especially to the Heaven Plate on the feng shui compass although they are also used on the Earth and Man Plates.

Stems being connected with water are used by the feng shui *hsien-sheng* to estimate the quality of, or the breaks, turns, junctions, points of appearance and points of disappearance of watercourses visible from the prospective *hsueh*. The Stems are in fact sometimes referred to as "containing water." Remember that even in the West the phrase "milky way" applies to the stars showing an unacknowledged connection between them and water or milk. The Egyptians also saw the stars as the milk from the breasts of Nuit, goddess of the sky.

Table 10. *The ten Heavenly Stems*

Number	Name		Element
1	甲	*chia*	Wood
2	乙	*i*	
3	丙	*ping*	Fire
4	丁	*ting*	
5	戊	*wu*	Earth
6	己	*chi*	
7	庚	*keng*	Metal
8	辛	*hsin*	
9	壬	*jen*	Water
10	癸	*kuei*	

In some (San He) feng shui formulas, four of the Stems are considered lucky, and four unlucky.

Unlucky Stems	Lucky Stems
1	3
2	4
9	7
10	8

The relative luck of the Stems, in the context of this formula, is related to their association with the trigrams, the unlucky Stems in this case being associated with the Ch'ien and K'un trigrams which are unlucky because they are overwhelmingly yang and yin respectively, with no admixture.

Contrarily, because Stems 3, 4, 7, and 8 are associated with the Ken and Hsun trigrams, which have a suitable mixture of yin and yang, they are lucky.

Stems 1 and 9 are considered as "yang orphans," that is, children left alone in the world who therefore need to extend their own self-reliance in a very yang way.

Stems 2 and 10 are "yin emptiness": quite the reverse, but again an undesirable state, with no balancing yang. Orphan-emptiness literally means "unlucky" in Chinese.

Stems 3 and 7 are yang prosperity. Here the lucky Stems have a good blend of yin and yang. "Prosperity-assistance" is the Chinese compound word for "lucky."

Stems 4 and 8 are "yin assistance," again a lucky blend.

Stems 5 and 6 stand for the center and do not partake of any particular direction. On the scale of numbers 1 to 10 they also stand at the middle, 5 and 6 being respectively half of the Stems and half of the Branches. They are also allocated to no trigram, as of course there are only eight trigrams to go with ten Stems. They are therefore referred to as "tortoiseshell." As such, they therefore have no business with any specific *ch'i*. They may, if anything, be unlucky, but they are more correctly thought of as negative rather than unlucky, in that they may be used in a fairly esoteric way to control the dispersal of *sha* (noxious vapors), by imposing the rule of the tortoise on the *sha* to dispatch it to its proper place.

The Heavenly Stems, like the Earthly Branches, also do service in other ways, and often stand for the numerals 1 to 10, or grouped, in yin-yang pairs, stand for the five Elements.

12 The Twelve Earthly Branches

The twelve Earthly Branches give specific information about time or place. The twelve main points on the compass are those allocated to the twelve Earthly Branches, and their basic function is to mark the terrestrial directions. They are basically more at home on the Earth and Man Plates of the compass than on the Heaven Plate. They mark the location of earth dragon *ch'i*.

Taken on their own the Branches also indicate the twelve double-hour divisions of the day as well as the twelve months of the year, so they are the "alphabet" used to measure space and time.

The Branches have come to be used as time markers for anything involving a fraction of twelve, including the Great

Table 11. The twelve Earthly Branches

Chinese	12 Earthly Branches	Symbolic animal	Month	Double-hour of the day	Direction
子	*Tzu*	Rat	mid-winter	11 p.m.–1 a.m.	N
丑	*Ch'ou*	Ox	late winter	1 a.m.–3 a.m.	N30°E
寅	*Yin*	Tiger	early spring	3 a.m.–5 a.m.	N60°E
卯	*Mao*	Hare	mid-spring	5 a.m.–7 a.m.	E
辰	*Ch'en*	Dragon	late spring	7 a.m.–9 a.m.	S60°E
巳	*Ssu*	Snake	early summer	9 a.m.–11 a.m.	S30°E
午	*Wu*	Horse	mid-summer	11 a.m.–1 p.m.	S
未	*Wei*	Sheep	late summer	1 p.m.–3 p.m.	S30°W
申	*Shen*	Monkey	early autumn	3 p.m.–5 p.m.	S60°W
酉	*Yu*	Cock	mid-autumn	5 p.m.–7 p.m.	W
戌	*Hsu*	Dog	late autumn	7 p.m.–9 p.m.	N60°W
亥	*Hai*	Boar	early winter	9 p.m.–11 p.m.	N30°W

Year, the duration of Jupiter's revolution around the Sun, of twelve ordinary years.

Hence a year, a month, and a (Chinese) hour (of 120 minutes) can all be designated by one of the twelve Earthly Branches, which can then in turn signify a direction of the compass for each of these times, providing more mechanics for correlating space and time. The correlations are shown in table 11, in which the Branches are correlated to animals used in simple Chinese astrology as year designations.

The seasons fit in naturally with the Branches and indicate the best times of the year for initiating projects connected with building or buying. The winter solstice occurs half way through Branch *tzu* (due north), and the rest of the Branches follow in order allocating the parts of the compass to the time of the year through *mao,* due east; *wu,* due south (midsummer); and *yu,* due west (autumn).

The twelve Earthly Branches are not confined to Earth because when taken with the ten Heavenly Stems they become the sixty sexagenary characters.

60 The Sexagenary Characters

The sexagenary character series is made up by combining the ten Heavenly Stems with the twelve Earthly Branches of the same sex. In Chinese these are referred to as the *chia tzu,* because this is the first combination of Stem and Branch. In fact only the yang Earthly Branches are combined with the yang Heavenly Stems, and vice versa. This way sixty sexagenary character combinations result, instead of the 120 that would occur without the same-sex limitation that odd must be paired with odd, and even paired with even.

On the *lo p'an,* the sexagenary characters are also called "dragons" because they are used to trace the earth *ch'i* dragon veins flowing through the ground. They also provide the key as to the time of the year at which a particular vein may be "opened" to a site. Regardless of which compass Ring to use, the attributions of "lucky" and "unlucky" to the various sexagenary characters is fairly consistent, there being only minor differences between the Rings. Of these, exactly half the dragons/sexagenary characters are lucky and half unlucky. For example the dragons exactly on the center of each of the twenty-four directions are considered unlucky because they represent a too strong and therefore unbalanced energy.

Like the twelve Branches, which represent a twelve-year cycle, the sexagenary characters represent a sixty-year cycle. It is this cycle that provides each Chinese year with its designation of Element and Animal, like the year of the Wooden Rat or the year of the Metal Dragon. In each case the animal is derived from one of the twelve Earthly Branches and the Element from one of the five pairs of Heavenly Stems that go into making up the sexagenary characters. These designations are popular in Chinese astrology. For a more thorough *pa tzu (Ba Zi)* reading, the sexagenary characters of the hour, day, and month must be added to the year of birth to construct a complete horoscope.

24 The Chinese Solar Calendar and 24 Mini-Seasons

The moon determines the length of each month, but the year's length is governed by the sun. However, the solar year cannot be evenly divided up by lunar months. There are therefore two quite distinct Chinese calendars, the lunar calendar and the solar calendar. The solar calendar is the one used in feng shui, and it includes many of the categories so far considered.

The twenty-four divisions of the farmer's calendar, or solar calendar, which are sometimes referred to as mini-seasons, are used to this day in China. The calendar is divided into twelve *chieh* (節) and twelve *ch'i* (氣). *Chieh* and *ch'i* are roughly the same, except *chieh* mark the beginning of one of the parts of the year, i.e., the beginning of a season, a solstice, or an equinox. Each of the *chieh/ch'i* correspond to 15 degrees of the sun's movement along the ecliptic and is therefore approximately equal to fifteen to sixteen days.

The year is thus divided into twenty-four *chieh/ch'i*. It is also subdivided into seventy-two *hou* (three for each *chieh/ ch'i*). This means that each *hou* is slightly more than five days long. These are used to determine the correct time to do certain building work or to make certain feng shui changes.

The duration of these twenty-four divisions of the solar calendar are defined exactly to the hour and minute. Their dates appear to fluctuate by a few days from year to year. This incidentally is not due to imprecision in the Chinese calendar, but to the imprecision of the Western Gregorian calendar caused by leap year interpolations.

Table 12. The twenty-four divisions of the solar year

Name in Chinese	English meaning	Approx. date begins
Li ch'un	Beginning of spring	4 Feb.
Yu shui	Rain water	19 Feb.
Ching chih	Excited insects	6 March
Ch'un fen	*Spring Equinox*	21 March
Ch'ing ming	Clear and bright	5 April
Ku yu	Grain rain	21 April
Li hsia	Summer begins	6 May
Hsiao man	Grain filling	21 May
Mang chung	Grain in ear	6 June
Hsia chih	*Summer Solstice*	22 June
Hsiao shu	Slight heat	7 July
Ta shu	Great heat	23 July
Li ch'iu	Autumn begins	8 Aug.
Ch'u shu	Limit of heat	24 Aug.
Pai lu	White dew	8 Sept.
Ch'iu fen	*Autumn Equinox*	23 Sept.
Han lu	Cold dew	8 Oct.
Shuang chiang	Hoarfrost descends	24 Oct.
Li tung	Winter begins	7 Nov.
Hsiao hsueh	Slight snow	23 Nov.
Ta hsueh	Great snow	7 Dec.
Tung chih	*Winter Solstice*	22 Dec.
Hsiao han	Slight cold	6 Jan.
Ta han	Great cold	21 Jan.

The climatic descriptions fit the weather of northern China, the likely origin of this division. The twenty-four solar divisions of the year also have spatial equivalents. The compass links them to the twenty-four directions (see Table 14), and thus it integrates time and space considerations into a single series of symbols. If the twenty-four points are paired into twelve, each pair contains one Branch, and the disposition of Branches is the same in the rings of twenty-four points as it is in the compass rings of sexagenary characters. The sexagenary characters therefore are an elaboration of both the twenty-four points and the twenty-four solar divisions of time. In short, feng shui bridges space and time using the compass to interpret both.

In San He School practice, this gives a significance to one particular direction at a particular time of the year. It is for this reason that burial or building is often put off for many months, for although a suitable site may have been found, it is necessary to wait until the time of the year coincides with the site's orientation. To show how culturally ingrained this is, these dates are now part of the standard software supplied with Nokia mobile phones in Southeast Asia.

The Chinese Lunar Calendar

In opposition to the practical farming "real" solar calendar is the Imperial Calendar, which is based on the lunar cycles of twenty-nine or thirty days.

In order to keep the lunar calendar abreast of the solar calendar, you have to insert intercalary lunar months in every so many years. When the winter solstice fell near the last day of the eleventh lunar month, an intercalary month was ordained by the Imperial Calendar-makers for the following year. Lunar months were numbered but not named. Intercalary lunar months took the number of the preceding lunar month, so that the twelfth month always falls somewhere between January and February.

As the lunar calendar is the sacred calendar according to which many annual festivals are timed, it is not the calendar of agricultural use, because the lunar months do not fall at the same time each year. Farmers use the solar calendar (or *Hsia* calendar) to time the agricultural cycle, as is indicated by the names of the *ch'i/chieh* periods. The solar calendar is also the calendar used by feng shui practitioners to determine the changes in the Flying Stars over time. For keeping historical records a third way of dating was used, and that is the reign date of the emperor or, as it is now, the year of the Republic or People's Republic.

The solar calendar provides the basis for astrological calculations that link individuals to specific sites. The importance of the personal equation in relation to a particular site is sometimes overlooked. If a feng shui *hsien-sheng* is assessing a site for a building project, then he has to know the date and time of birth of the owner. If he is, however, examining a tomb or yin dwelling, he has to know the birth date and death date of the person to be buried. This date is then correlated, using the Chinese Almanac, the *Tung Sing* or *Tung Shu*, with the directions of the feng shui compass to find the correct orientation. The *Tung Sing* relates the month and year of birth to the Chinese animal symbolic of that month and year, an order that is repeated every twelve years cyclically, the full cycle taking five groups of twelve, i.e., sixty years in all.

These animal symbols are related to the direction of the compass according to the table of the twelve Earthly Branches, which also takes into account the time of day most appropriate for initiating any action associated with a particular direction. Conjunctions or actions may be found, in fact, which neutralize such dangers. But if it is not possible to discover them, the family is constrained to put off the burial until the almanac assigns another direction as peculiarly auspicious. On the connection between individual horoscopes and feng shui practice, a short quote from De Groot (1897:976) gives an excellent example:

These [sexagenary] characters being firmly believed to determine his fate for ever, no burial place can answer to the geomantic [feng shui] requirements if the cyclical characters expressing the year of the birth of the occupant stand in the compass on the lower end of the line which the almanac has decreed as auspicious for the current year and in which, of course, the coffin is to be placed. Suppose, for instance, this line runs from south to north, so that the longitudinal axis of the grave should fall within the segment defined on the compass by the limits of the point [*tzu*] or the north, as indicated on the [compass] circles [Rings] VI and VIII [see Figure 19]. If then the dead man has been born in a year denoted by a binomium [the Sexagenary characters or combined Stem and Branch of the year] in which the character [*tzu*] occurs, his horoscope is deemed to collide with the good influences that flow from south to north and to neutralize their benefits, and no blessings can ever be expected from his grave if it is placed in this direction. Hence its axis must be shifted a little [one Direction or 15 degrees] to the right or left, without, however, going beyond the northern quadrant; and if it is feared that the beneficial influences of the auspicious line will in this way be lost, the burial must be postponed. The month, day and hour of the birth of the deceased may cause similar collisions, though they are of a less dangerous nature, such dates forming the less important parts of his horoscope.

120 The 120 *Fen-chin* or "Golden Divisions"

Although the Chinese characters for *fen-chin* literally translate as "gold division," it is more correct to just refer to them as "divisions" and not by the elaborate names used by some writers on feng shui, like "bags of gold." This cycle is an extension of the sexagenary characters. On a small compass it is difficult to site a particular feature just using the red thread so that it lies unequivocally on one of the *fen-chin* unless one has eyes like telescope sights, so some feng shui masters use a theodolite to take accurate measurements.

Table 13. *The twenty-eight hsiu with the cardinal directions highlighted*

No.	Chinese	Constellation in Wade-Giles	English translation	Number of degrees extent (basis 365.25) Chinese degrees	Starting degree (basis 360 degrees) counting counterclockwise
Azure Dragon Quarter					
1	角	Chiao	Horn	12.75	113.60
2	亢	K'ang	Neck	9.75	103.98
3	氐	Ti	Base/root	16.25	87.96
4	**房**	**Fang**	**Room**	**5.75**	**82.30**
5	心	Hsin	Heart	6.00	76.38
6	尾	Wei	Tail	18.00	58.64
7	箕	Chi	Sieve/winnowing basket	9.50	49.28
Black Tortoise Quarter					
8	斗	Tou	Dipper/measure	22.75	26.85
9	牛	Niu	Oxherd boy	7.00	19.96
10	女	Nu	Maiden	11.00	9.11
11	**虛**	**Hsu**	**Void**	**9.25**	**0.00**
12	危	Wei	Danger (rooftop)	16.00	344.23
13	室	Shih	House	18.25	326.24
14	壁	Pi	Wall	9.75	316.63

Table 13. The twenty-eight hsiu with the cardinal directions highlighted

No.	Chinese	Constellation in Wade-Giles	English translation	Number of degrees extent (basis 365.25 Chinese degrees)	Starting degree (basis 360 degrees) counting counterclockwise
White Tiger Quarter					
15	奎	K'uei	Astride	18.00	298.89
16	婁	Lou	Mound/tether	12.75	286.32
17	胃	Wei	Stomach	15.25	271.29
18	**昴**	**Mao**	**Pleiades constellation**	**11.00**	**260.45**
19	畢	Pi	Conclusion or graduation	16.50	244.19
20	觜	Tsui	Beak/turtle	0.50	243.69
21	參	Shen	Crossing/mixture	9.50	234.33
Red Bird Quarter					
22	井	Ching	Well	30.25	204.51
23	鬼	Kuei	Ghost	2.50	202.05
24	柳	Liu	Willow	13.50	188.74
25	**星**	**Hsing**	**[Seven] Stars**	**6.75**	**182.09**
26	張	Chang	Spread (e.g., bow or net)	17.75	164.50
27	翼	I	Wings	20.25	144.64
28	軫	Chen	Carriage seat	18.75	126.16
				365.25	

Likewise in the practice of feng shui, the idea that one can be as accurate as one *fen-chin* division, that is 3 degrees, by eye, when trying to sight the top of a mountain five miles away with a bit of thread and two weights, is difficult to believe. In addition, small compass needles, some being only an inch or so long, make it difficult to guarantee precise readings.

Some simplified versions of the feng shui compass exclude the sixty sexagenary characters. However if they are omitted, it becomes difficult to establish whether a specific vein of *ch'i* is waxing or waning. When a bearing is taken ascribed to one of the sexagenary characters, the state of the *ch'i* in that feature of the landscape can be determined, and the six-day period of the year appropriate to the feature can also be obtained. If it is decided to connect the influence of the feature being sited to the potential *hsueh*, dragon's lair, then burial or building is not executed until those six days come around. This way a certain vein of *ch'i* can be tapped from the surrounding landscape above all other veins, and this vein will continue to supply the *hsueh* with *ch'i* from thenceforth.

28 The Twenty-eight *Hsiu* (宿) or Mansions of the Moon

Other series can be found on the outer rim of most *lo p'ans*. The most common is the twenty-eight unevenly spaced constellations or Mansions of the Moon, which, as they reflect the irregularities of the night sky, do not dovetail mathematically with any of the other cosmological categories.

The moon was seen to pass through the Mansions, or *hsiu*, "residing" in each for a given number of days. Hence, their length is measured in 365.25 Chinese degrees, rather than the Western 360 degrees. Arabs and Indian astronomers also have twenty-eight Mansions of the Moon, but these are of equal length. The Chinese are the only culture to have unevenly lengthed Mansions of the Moon.

The twenty-eight *hsiu* are asterisms, or minor constellations, whose approximate position in the sky and the stars
they include are given in Table 13.

The identification of the *hsiu* was first made about 2400 BC,
and traditionally they formed a rough belt around the
equator. In the course of time they have physically moved
some distance from their former positions, but the areas of
sky where they used to be located are still referred to as the
hsiu. Thus the heavens are divided into twenty-eight uneven-
sized segments arrayed in the same order.

Some of the animals associated with the *hsiu* have been
appropriated by the twelve Earthly Branches as their particular symbol. These symbols will sometimes coincide with the
interpretations of the Form School of feng shui, which may
see a hill shaped like a turtle and refer it to that part of the
compass occupied by the constellation Tsui.

Although Eitel refers to the *hsiu* as "signs of the zodiac," this
identification is definitely *not* correct, and "Mansions of the
Moon" would be a much better translation. Besides, the *hsiu*
are measured along the Earth's equator not along the ecliptic,
as are the signs of the zodiac. The *hsiu*, like the zodiac, refer to
stars that, by the procession of the equinoxes, have now moved
away from their original spot, while the *hsiu* or sign name still
persists in being attributed to that part of the sky: this they
have in common.

The *hsiu* together with the other cosmological categories
considered in this chapter make up the building blocks of the
feng shui compass. An understanding of these makes it possible to understand the compass as a rich indicator of the direction and quality of *ch'i* flow entering, leaving, and affecting a
site. When used in conjunction with their temporal meanings,
appropriate times can be ascertained for influencing these
ch'i flows to benefit the overall energy balance of a site, be it
a whole town, village, home, or single room.

5
Pivot of the Four Quarters: Compass School

As to the Earth, the east-west direction is the weft and the north-south direction the warp.

—*Ta Tai Li Chi*

Magnetism and Living Creatures

Biological work done in the late 1970s indicates that certain bacteria swim in the northern hemisphere northward and in the southern hemisphere southward along the lines of the Earth's magnetic field. Their inbuilt sensors that respond to the field are in fact made of a form of magnetite: almost "organic magnets." Although this was heralded as a new discovery, it was known to the Chinese in the first century AD. Wang Chung said in the *Lung Heng* (Chapter 52 [ch. 17, p. 4a]): "So also certain maggots which arise from fish and meat, placed on the ground, move northward. This is the nature of these maggots. If indeed the 'indicator-plant' moved or pointed, that also was its nature given to it by Heaven" (translation by Needham, 1962, vol. 4, part I, p. 262).

Certainly, the Chinese knew of the magnetic effect of the Earth's gravitational field on animals, which they possibly attributed to the movement of *ch'i* through the earth, and so it was a logical development to conclude that the same field also affected human beings. Further biological work currently being undertaken does seem in fact to support this theory as more and more members of the animal kingdom have their inbuilt sensitivity to the magnetic field discovered.

The earliest formal recognition of the effect the Earth's field has upon organic life is found in the writings of the Fukien [Fujian] School of feng shui.

The Fukien [Fujian] School, which is frequently styled the "House and Dwellings Method" or the "Method of Man," claims as its patriarch Wang Chih and is primarily attached to the use of the feng shui compass.

Feng Shui and the Maritime Use of the *Lo p'an*

The use of the compass for feng shui purposes definitely predated its maritime use, and for the feng shui *hsien-sheng* the compass has always been an instrument of the land not the sea. The adoption of the compass by Chinese sailors (circa tenth century AD) was in fact probably long retarded by its feng shui use (beginning before the seventh century AD), and by the fact that throughout the Middle Ages, Chinese river and canal traffic predominated over ocean voyages. It was often said that the needle of the feng shui compass is best fitted for determining the flow of the *ch'i* in the Earth because it has been magnetized by direct contact with the Earth *ch'i* of a lodestone and is therefore able to seek the Earth *ch'i* out. It is for this reason also that the inner Rings of the compass, called the Earth Plate, align exactly with the loadstone-activated needle.

In about AD 300 the feng shui master Kuo P'o used the words (translated by Needham [1962, vol. 4, part 1:233]): "The lodestone 'breathes in' [attracts] iron, and amber collects mustard-seeds [by electrostatic attraction]. The *ch'i* (of these things) has an invisible penetratingness, rapidly effecting a mysterious contact, according to the mutual responses of things." The Chinese were aware that both the Earth's magnetic field and electrostatic attraction acted at a distance, but thought (not unreasonably) that their nature was similar.

Such a lodestone or needle will certainly be deflected from true magnetic north by local ferro-nickel deposits, thereby effectively reflecting variations in local geology rather than always being oriented in the same direction.

The relationship between the feng shui and maritime use of the compass is illustrated by the *Chiu T'ien Hsuan Nu Ch'ing-nang Hai-chiao Ching* ("The Nine Heavens Mysterious Girl's Universe [literally 'blue bag'] and Sea Corner Classic"), sometimes attributed to Kuo P'o (AD 276–324), but probably dating from soon after Yang Yun Sung. The title, which has been variously translated, is revealing because it refers to the Universe as the "blue bag," an indication of strong Taoist associations, and to the "sea angle" or "ocean corner," probably indicating either the "new" maritime use for the *lo p'an*, or highlighting the four corner trigrams embedded in the twenty-four Mountains.

The "Mysterious Girl" of the title is Hsuan Nu, who, "in the daytime . . . determined the [sailing] directions [of the compass] by the rising and setting of the sun. In the night she determined the directions by the divisions of the *hsiu*," or in other words, she behaved just as sailors have for centuries. However, with the invention of the "south-pointer," "a copper plate was made with exactly twenty-four Mountains [chosen from] the ten Heavenly Stems [that had been associated with the] Heaven Plate [*t'ien p'an*] [of Han dynasty diviner's board or *shih*], and the twelve Earthly Branches [that had been associated with the] Earth Plate [*ti p'an*] [of the diviner's board]." The former are called *li hsiang na shui* and the latter *ko lung shou sha*.

European and Chinese Divisions of the Compass

The Chinese incidentally always thought of the compass as south-pointing, in deference to their use of south as the prime cardinal point. The other end of course points north, so the difference is only semantic and not real. When considering only the cardinal points in relation to the European compass no difficulty arises except the necessity of drawing maps as if standing with one's back to the north, facing southward.

When examining the intercardinal points, we find that the Chinese divide these differently. The Western approach is always to refer to a point, and to divide the compass by successive halving of divisions. The European arrangement produces divisions into:

N, S, E, W at intervals of 90 degrees
N, NE, E, at intervals of 45 degrees
N, NNS, NE, ENE, E, at intervals of 22.5 degrees
N, N by E, NNE, NE by N, NE, NE by E, ENE, E by N,
    E at intervals of 11.5 degrees

The Chinese feng shui practitioner on the other hand divides the compass into twenty-four divisions, that is, at intervals of 15 degrees. It is impossible therefore to indicate which *segments* are meant by using the *points* of European nomenclature. Edkins (1872) was the first to fall into this trap. Subsequent writers have compounded Edkin's mistake, and Evelyn Lip (1979:19) also applies unevenly spaced European compass *points* to evenly spaced Chinese compass *segments*. While European compass points are just that, Chinese compass bearings refer to a *segment* of the circle not a specific *point* on its circumference.

The feng shui compass is not only divided by twenty-four but has a number of different "Rings" split up according to the different requirements and formulas; with division by eight, twenty-four, sixty, seventy-two, and so on, all equally unsuited to description in terms of European compass points. The compass is thus not only a feng shui aid but a pocket guide to Chinese philosophy, astronomy, astrology, and cosmology because it contains in its many Rings (sometimes as many as thirty-eight) a complete summary of all the major categories and divisions of these subjects.

The *Lo P'an*

The compass itself is called the *lo p'an* (羅盤), or *luo pan*. *Lo* can mean a conch or screw-like shape, a spiral. Loosely applied to the concentric rings of the compass-plate it implies that they radiate out from the center or Heaven Pool. Sometimes the *lo p'an* is referred to as a *ti lo* or "earth spiral," while in the Amoy [Xiamen] dialect it is called *lo ching* (羅經), or *luo jing*, which De Groot translates as "reticular tissue," as the sectors and concentric circles reminded him of a net.

Physically the *lo p'an* is a circular disc of wood, averaging six to eight inches across and rounded at the bottom like a solid saucer. It is usually set in a square board symbolic of the Earth, which is used when aligning it. The upper surface is divided into concentric circles called *ts'eng* (層), or *ceng* ("stories" or "layers"), and is flat except for the small depression in the center, the "Heaven Pool," which contains a magnetized needle, usually less than an inch in length, which has its red end pointing to the south while its other end seeks magnetic north. It usually has a glass cover. A line drawn on the bottom of the needle house is aligned with the needle to oriente the *lo p'an* on a north-south bearing.

The *lo p'an* is often lacquered or painted yellow on the top surface, black lacquered underneath, and inscribed with black, red, or gold characters, the whole being varnished to protect it. More modern *lo p'ans* (especially those made in Taiwan) are precision instruments, each often made to the specifications of one master. Such *lo p'ans* are available in Hong Kong, Singapore, Malaysia, and mainland China, but as yet the quality of those made in the People's Republic is not up to the standard of those made in Hong Kong or Taiwan, and they are mostly simply decorative. The number of rings on the *lo p'an* varies with the size and cost of the instrument. The reverse side usually has a square-gridded table, which holds the essence of the Eight Mansion formula and sometimes a listing of the various rings.

Although there is much variety, the arrangement of feng shui *lo p'ans* follows basically the same pattern, the number of rings being in the region of eight to thirty-eight. The most comprehensive work on a compass, the *Lo Ching Chieh* or "Explanation of the Compass" by Wu Wang Kang, defines the contents of each ring, beginning at the center and working outward. The various rings incorporate not only consistent sets of symbolism but also other cosmological systems. Some rings are based on a division of 365.25 days, some on 360 degrees, others on the twenty-eight *hsiu* (lunar Mansions) or the sixty or seventy-two dragons.

One ring that always occurs near the center of every *lo p'an* is the eight trigrams that indicate the cardinal points, and the "corner" or intercardinal points between them. Another common ring divides into the twenty-four directional points, which are also used on Chinese mariners' compasses. Beyond this, the compass is divided into sixty sectors, then 120, and finally 360 (or 365.25), the number of degrees in the full circle (or days in the year).

There are other cycles involved as mentioned above, but the main divisions can all be expressed as multiples of the five Elements and the twelve Earthly Branches:

Heavenly Stems	$10 = 2 \times 5$ (the 5 Elements*)
Earthly Branches	$12 = 12 \times 1$
Directional points (Mountains)	$24 = 12 \times 2$
Sexagenary characters	$60 = 12 \times 5$
Dragons	$72 = 12 \times 6$
Fen-chin	$120 = 12 \times 10$
Degrees in a circle	$360 = 12 \times 30$
Days in a year	365.25 (total number of degrees in the twenty-eight *hsiu*)

* Although the Earth Element is not used.

The compass is thus firmly based on multiples of twelve: the twelve Earthly Branches, the twelve months of the year, and the twelve double-hours of the day. The five Elements and eight of the ten Stems interact with the Branches throughout the whole cycle.

The Diviner's Board or *Shih* (式)

Joseph Needham had a theory that attempts to explain the origin of divining boards and from these the *lo p'an*. He suggested that early divining boards were used as fields upon which were thrown the divining instruments. These formed the patterns of the constellations, revealing which constellations were operating on what earthly conditions at any particular moment, much in the manner of casting *I Ching* hexagrams for an estimate of the changes operative at a particular moment.

This diviner's board (*shih*) in fact was much more sophisticated and complex than this, with an upper circular disk rotated upon its lower square plate, with time and space markers that aligned with each other as it turned. It was made of bronze or lacquered wood and consisted of a round plate representing the Heavens mounted above a square board symbolizing the Earth. This circular model of the cosmos was marked with the *hsiu*, astronomical signs, and characters to represent the days, months, and years. The lower Earth Plate was marked with the twenty four directions and the twelve Earthly Branches.

In the center of the circular "Heaven Plate" was a drawing of the Big Dipper, or Northern Ladle, a part of Ursa Major (Great Bear), which is the constellation in the northern sky that rotates around the Polestar and acts as a seasonal pointer. In the divination process, the court diviner would turn the circular "Heaven Plate" on its axis in imitation of the movement of the Big Dipper around the Polestar according to the seasons. This was the time element that was then related to the directional element, represented by the square Earth Plate. While the *shih* might have been a precursor of the *lo p'an*, it is more likely to have had a completely different usage associated with *tai yi* or *chi men tun chia* divination rather than feng shui, because it did *not*, at this point anyway, incorporate the magnetic needle that is essential for feng shui.

Wang Chen-To (in 1948 and 1951) hypothesized that the drawing of the Big Dipper constellation was perhaps later replaced by an actual ladle or magnetized spoon made of wood, stone, or pottery. Although Needham also endorsed this idea, it is not in fact true, and was simply a theory prompted by the presence of a shattered (nonmagnetic) spoon that happened to be found in the same archaeological dig as an early diviner's board. It is safe to disregard the swiveling spoon theory, even though it has been repeated by endless writers ever since. In fact small-scale models of this totally fallacious device are being sold in increasingly large numbers. Derek Walters, in his excellent book *Chinese Astrology*, has made the same observation about the fallaciousness of this supposition.

Let us look at the diviner's board in its original shape (without magnetized revolving spoons). Needham (1962, vol. 4, part 1, pp. 262–3) describes the diviner's board as:

> composed of two boards or plates, the lower one being square (to symbolise the earth, hence called the *ti p'an*); and the upper one being round (to symbolise heaven, hence called the *t'ien p'an*). The latter revolved on a central pivot and had engraved upon it the 24 compass points, composed, just as in the later traditional compass, of the denary [Heavenly Stems] and duodenary [Earthly Branches] cyclical characters, *wu* and *chi* (which symbolised the earth) being repeated in order to make up the full number. It always bore, engraved at the center, a representation of the Great Bear. The "ground-plate" was marked all about its edge with the names of the 28 *hsiu* (equatorial divisions of constellations), and the 24 directions were repeated along its inner gradations. Moreover, it carried the eight chief *kua* (trigrams) arranged according to the *Hou T'ien* system so that *Chhien* [Ch'ien] occupied the north-west and *K'un* the southeast [in the Later Heaven Sequence]. This . . . differs from that found on all later geomantic compasses where *Chhien* [Ch'ien] is the south and *K'un* the north [in the Former Heaven Sequence].

It has also been possible to determine what the board was made of, as Needham continues (op. cit., p. 265):

> Something is known of the wood from which the *shih* were usually made in later times. The "Thang Liu T'ien"

("Institutions of the Tang Dynasty") from between +713 and +755 [AD] states that the round "heaven-plate" was made of maple wood, and the square "ground-plate" of selected jujube wood.

It seems possible that the diviner's board, or *shih,* was in fact the forerunner of the feng shui *lo p'an* with its square Earth base into which the circular disc is set.

The Magnetic Needle

However, before the *shih* can become a *lo p'an* it needs the addition of a mounted magnetic needle which is at the heart of feng shui. When the ancient Chinese learned how to induce or transfer magnetism from magnetite to pieces of iron, they began to make a magnetic pointer in the shape of an iron fish, or tadpole, which floated on water. Eventually (possibly as early as the fourth century AD) the iron was shaped into a needle, or an experimenter magnetized a stitching needle. The use of the needle shape enabled much greater directional precision in reading.

In all probability, from the beginning of its use at sea, sometime between 850 and 1050, the compass was a magnetized needle floating on water in a small hollow. Among the oldest types that have been found are flat bronze plates six inches or less in diameter with a bowl-shaped depression in the center where the needle floated. Chinese navigators remained faithful to floating compasses of one kind or another until the last part of the sixteenth century when the dry-pivoted compass was introduced (with an attached compass card showing European directions) to East Asia by Dutch or Portuguese seamen. But long before this the compass was well established as a feng shui tool.

The proof of the primacy of the compass as a feng shui tool before becoming a maritime aid is to be found in a manuscript that contains a liturgical form for use in the ship's chapel or before the compass at the beginning of a voyage.

The litany incorporates as saints and sages the names of a number of feng shui *hsien-sheng* both legendary and real. These include Ch'ing-Wu Tzu (the Blue Raven Master), Pai Ho Tzu (the White Crane Master), and Yang Chiu-P'in (another name for Yang Yun Sung in his guise as "rescuer of the poor," a reference to his ability to improve even the feng shui of the poor).

In an introduction written by Li Yu-Heng in 1570 for Ch'ing Wu's classic, he confirmed the change from floating to dry-pivoted compass:

> The needle floating on water and giving the north and south directions, is ordinarily called the Wet Compass (*shui lo ching*). In the Chia-Ch'ing reign-period (1522–66) there were attacks of Japanese pirates [on the coast], so from that time onward Japanese methods began to be used. Thus the needle was placed in the compass box, and a paper was stuck on to it carrying all the directions, so that no matter what direction is taken the *tzu* (north) and *wu* (south) signs are always situated at the north and south. This is called the Dry Compass (*han lo ching*).

Feng shui was thus the mother of the systematic use of magnetism in navigation and geography, just as astrology was the mother of astronomy, and alchemy of chemistry.

It is only one short step from the *shih* to inserting a needle well into its circular disc so that it still rotates on or within the square Earth Plate. The rings from the *shih* formed the oldest "layer" of the *lo p'an*.

Twenty-four Mountains (二十四山)

The next oldest Ring is probably that of the twenty-four directions. Let us look more closely at this Ring of twenty-four directions. These twenty-four directions are poetically called "Mountains" although they have no direct connection with any physical mountains. Although this is confusing, it has become the standard feng shui terminology to call these twenty-four directions *shan* (山) or "Mountains."

The key to the function of each Plate is to be found in the twenty-four Mountains. These are not made up of an internally consistent set of symbols, but are formed from three other groups of symbols, used alternately:

4 of the 8 trigrams used as intercardinal (corner) points
8 of the 10 Heavenly Stems (omitting the two Earth Stems)
12 Earthly Branches
—
24

These are evenly disposed on the *lo p'an* as shown in Table 14. The table shows that the twenty-four Mountains divide the circle into segments of 15 degrees. The Earthly Branches are fully represented, but the Heavenly Stems have lost *wu* and *chi*, the Stems relating to the Earth. This omission leaves four "corner" places, which are filled by the four most important *kua*, or trigrams.

This is clearly described in Yang Yun-Sung's *Ch'ing Nang Ao-Chih* ("Mysterious Principles of the Blue Bag" [a poetic name for the Universe]). The omission may have been essentially practical, since the Chinese characters *wu* (戊) and *chi* (己) would so readily be confused with the characters *hsu* (戌) and *ssu* (巳), but it is more likely that as *wu* and *chi* symbolized the Element Earth, which is associated with the Center, therefore they were not available to be included among the twenty-four Mountains.

The characters used on the *lo p'an* are not the characters commonly used in China to represent directions. Their origin or etymology is, for the most part, lost in the mists of antiquity, but many of them date back over 4,000 years when they appeared on early oracle bones.

There are three main types of *lo p'an*:

1. San He
2. San Yuan
3. Mixed

Mixed *lo p'ans* are the most common, and they have rings from both the main schools. We will look at the San He *lo p'an* rings.

The Structure of the *Lo p'an*

Working from the center of the *lo p'an* outward we find that almost every *lo p'an* has the eight trigrams of the *I Ching* as its inmost ring. These are usually shown in the Former Heaven Sequence, in the ideal order. If one uses the analogy of the growth of tree rings, then this is probably the oldest ring or stratum. Certainly the eight trigrams appear by themselves in many octagonal or circular Chinese motifs, from the earliest times.

Analysis of the Rings

The sixteen-ring *lo p'an* that we are about to analyze and dissect is a nineteenth-century San He *lo p'an* that appears in De Groot (1892, vol. 3:958). When you look at a San He *lo p'an*, it is useful to pick out each of these Plate groupings from the start, as each performs a totally different feng shui function, and this makes the ring layout more easily comprehensible. The Rings of this *lo p'an* divide up as shown in Table 15. First look at Figure 19 where the whole *lo p'an* appears. We will pick out just one Mountain (a direction segment), due south (*wu*), and trace its occurrence across the three Plates. You can easily see why we approach the *lo p'an* by first just examining one of the Mountains (*wu*) rather than trying to digest it as a whole.

The Three Plates

The San He *lo p'an* has three groups of similar concentric Rings that are referred to as Plates. The inner Plate is called

Table 14. *The twenty-four Mountains or* lo p'an *directions*

DIRECTION	MOUNTAIN NAME	WHAT IT IS	YIN OR YANG	RANGE OF COMPASS DEGREES	CHINESE CHARACTER
	Ping	Stem	Yang	157.5-172.5	丙
South	**Wu**	**Branch**	**Yin**	**172.5-187.5**	午
	Ting	Stem	Yin	187.5-202.5	丁
	Wei	Branch	Yin	202.5-217.5	未
Southwest	**K'un**	**Trigram**	**Yang**	**217.5-232.5**	坤
	Shen	Branch	Yang	232.5-247.5	申
	Keng	Stem	Yang	247.5-262.5	庚
West	**Yu**	**Branch**	**Yin**	**262.5-277.5**	酉
	Hsin	Stem	Yin	277.5-292.5	辛
	Hsu	Branch	Yin	292.5-307.5	戌
Northwest	**Ch'ien**	**Trigram**	**Yang**	**307.5-322.5**	乾
	Hai	Branch	Yang	322.5-337.5	亥
	Jen	Stem	Yang	337.5-352.5	壬
North	**Tzu**	**Branch**	**Yin**	**352.5-7.5**	子
	Kuei	Stem	Yin	7.5-22.5	癸
	Ch'ou	Branch	Yin	22.5-37.5	丑
Northeast	**Ken**	**Trigram**	**Yang**	**37.5-52.5**	艮
	Yin	Branch	Yang	52.5-67.5	寅
	Chia	Stem	Yang	67.5-82.5	甲
East	**Mao**	**Branch**	**Yin**	**82.5-97.5**	卯
	I	Stem	Yin	97.5-112.5	乙
	Chen	Branch	Yin	112.5-127.5	辰
Southeast	**Sun**	**Trigram**	**Yang**	**127.5-142.5**	巽
	Ssu	Branch	Yang	142.5-157.5	巳

the Earth Plate. The outer Plate is the Heaven Plate. The Plate or group between them is the Man Plate (or if you prefer, the Human Plate). The Man Plate is sometimes unhelpfully (in Needham, for example) referred to as the "Inner Heaven Plate."

Now if either the ideal *lo p'an* of Wu Wang Kang, or the *lo p'an* used as an example in the next chapter (Figure 15) is closely scrutinized, it will be seen that the set of twenty-four Mountains are repeated on each of these three Rings.

However, the three Plates with these twenty-four Mountains are "staggered." Let us look at the *lo p'an* shown in Figure 15, and let us trace the occurrence and recurrence of just one of these twenty-four Mountains, the south point (marked by the character *wu*, 午). I have dissected this *lo p'an* just paying attention to this one Mountain in Figure 15. (In order to identify which ring we are talking about, it is important to count from the needle well including the well itself as Ring 1.)

The innermost occurrence of *wu* (the fourth Ring in our example in Figure 15) is the correct magnetic bearing for due south, while the next occurrence (the seventh Ring in our example) is 7.5 degrees to the left, and the third occurrence of this character (the ninth Ring) is 7.5 degrees to the right of the first occurrence.

It is not immediately obvious why three sets of identical Rings are needed, each 7.5 degrees out of phase with its fellows. Each of these Rings has a group of associated Rings attached, and it has become conventional to refer to these groups of Rings as "Plates." All San He *lo p'ans* have these three Plates.

Table 15. Typical division of the Rings into Plates (from center outward)

Ring	Ring numbers in Figure 15	
Needle well	1	
Eight trigrams	2–3	
Earth Plate	4–6	Correct Needle
Man Plate (or Inner Heaven Plate)	7–8	Central Needle
Heaven Plate	9–12	Seam Needle
Uneven divisions of five Elements	13	
The 365.25 days and degrees	14–15	
Twenty-eight *hsiu* or Mansions of the Moon	16	
360 degrees divisions	absent	

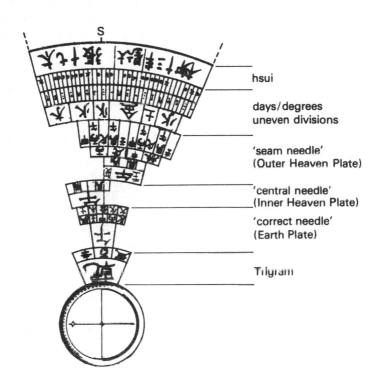

Figure 15. *The relative alignment of the south point on the three Plates*

The hsiu *and day/degree Rings*

Beyond the eight trigrams and the three Plates come the unevenly divided Rings that contain the five Elements spaced erratically (Ring 13) and then the twenty-eight *hsiu*, or constellations or Mansions of the Moon (Ring 16). The latter almost always form the penultimate Ring, and are recognizable as they are of variable angular length. The *hsiu* have been detailed at some length in Chapter 4.

Just inside the *hsiu* are often to be found several associated Rings with a complete breakdown of all the 360 degrees of the circle (post-Jesuit influenced) or more likely of the 365.25 days of the year. In the case of 365.25 divisions, a good or bad luck marking (red or black dot or cross) is often incorporated, allowing an evaluation of the feng shui quality of any direction in relation to every day of the year.

In the more complex *lo p'ans*, such as that of Wu Wang Kang, these Rings sometimes appear in other places on the *lo p'an* face as well, but in most *lo p'ans* they occupy the position next to the *hsiu*.

Beyond the *hsiu* is usually to be found the standard Western Ring of 360 degrees, although it does not exist in Figure 15.

The Historical Evolution of the Plates

According to tradition, the twenty-four Mountains were established in their present form at least by the time of Ch'iu Yen-Han, a geomancer who flourished in AD 713–741. They were aligned to the magnetic north-south axis and formed the inner or Earth Plate of the *lo p'an*, whose indictor was called the *Cheng Chen* or "Correct Needle."

The Cheng Chen *or "Correct Needle" (*正針*)*

The *Cheng Chen* is the name given to the *lo p'an* needle when it is used to read the Earth Plate. The basic twenty-four Mountains of the Earth Plate would have been sufficient for the basis of a single Plate compass, and also for all mariner's compasses.

The *Hai Chio Ching* explains that "nowadays feng shui practitioners use the *Cheng Chen* ("Correct Needle") and the Heaven-plate denary [Heavenly Stem] Mountains to find out where the dragon (*ko lung*) is." Thus the "Correct Needle" was used to locate the dragon, with the Stems and trigrams indicating the directions, while the Earthly Branches indicated the *ch'i* of the directions.

It seems likely that the inner Rings, including the eight trigrams (*pa kua*) plus the first set of twenty-four Mountains, formed the original core and totality of early *lo p'ans*. In fact the Chinese maritime compass, which was derived from the feng shui *lo p'an*, has to this day this simple form with just these twenty-four Mountains.

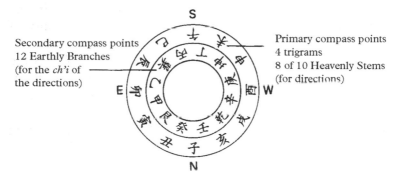

Secondary compass points
12 Earthly Branches
(for the *ch'i* of
the directions)

Primary compass points
4 trigrams
8 of 10 Heavenly Stems
(for directions)

Figure 16. The primary and secondary compass points

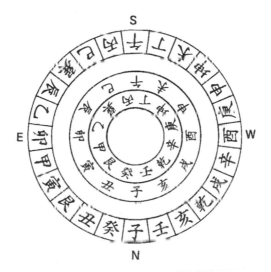

Figure 17. The full "Correct Needle"

The Feng Chen *or "Seam Needle" (* 縫針 *)*

The Seam Needle, or *Feng Chen,* is used to point to the outer
ring of twenty-four Mountains on the Heaven Plate. As the
Hai Chio Ching probably dates from shortly after the introduction of the Seam Needle, the latter is shown on Figure
18. The Rings are numbered in the traditional Chinese fashion
with the needle well counting as Ring 1.

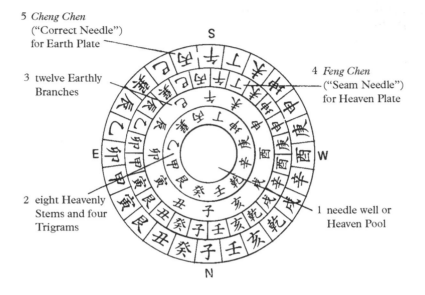

Figure 18. The "Correct" and "Seam" needles

In about AD 880 the great feng shui patriarch Yang Yun Sung added the Heaven Plate pointed to by the *Feng Chen* (not be confused with the 120 *fen-chin*). *Feng Chen* literally translates as "Seam Needle" or "stitching needle" and this Plate is deflected by 7.5 degrees east of north. When discussing the "Seam Needle" Needham incorrectly refers to it (1962, vol. 4, p. 304) as "magnetic north and south points," which of course it is not, being neither deflected to the same degree as the compass declination at the era of its inception, nor even in the same direction as current magnetic declination. Not only is it incorrect to refer to the "Seam Needle" as magnetic north and south (then or now), it is also misleading.

A clue to the reason behind the name "Seam Needle" is to be found in a discussion of steel needles in T'ao Ku's tenth-century *Ch'ing I Lu* (Chapter 2, p. 23b), which states that,

"Seamstresses or medical men will tell you the merits and disadvantages of different kinds of needles in just as much detail as Confucian scholars talking about brush pens." Perhaps Yang Yun Sung labeled his new arrangement the "Seam Needle" to impress upon his contemporaries its qualities.

The Chung Chen *or "Central Needle"* (中針)

Except for an angular displacement of 7.5 degrees the "Central Needle" is exactly the same as the Mountain Ring of the Correct Needle and the Seam Needle. Although both Central and Seam Needle overlap the Correct Needle, they do not overlap each other. The Central Needle is concerned with man-made landscape artifacts and so is logically "behind" the Seam Needle, which is concerned with Heaven and water.

In the twelfth century Master Lai introduced the third Plate, whose needle he referred to as the *Chung Chen* or "Central Needle," this time deviating 7.5 degrees west of north from the first or "Correct Needle." This is what he called the Man Plate (or Human Plate). It appears that this third addition was called the "Central Needle" because it is usually rather ignominiously sandwiched between the "Correct Needle" and the "Seam Needle."

If we take a slice through the *lo p'an* we get Figure 15. This cross section shows the relative position of just one of the twenty-four Mountains over each of the three Plates. In this example *wu*, the south point, has been chosen to illustrate the angular divergence of the three Plates. It is interesting that the Central Needle, or Man Plate, is relatively unimportant in terms of number of associated Rings (just one) on this example *lo p'an*.

There is of course only one physical needle per *lo p'an*, but it is referred to by one of its three possible titles, "Correct," "Seam" or "Central," according to which Plate (Earth, Heaven or Man respectively) is being read at the time. Table 16 summarizes the outward growth of the San He *lo p'an* so far.

Table 16. Historical development of the Rings of the lo p'an

Conventional Divisions of the Rings	Needle and Meaning	Declination	Established by	Date
Trigrams				Ancient
Earth Plate	*Cheng Chen—* "Correct Needle" 正針	magnetic north-south	before Ch'iu Yen-Han	before eighth century
Man (or Inner Heaven) Plate	*Chung Chen—* "Central Needle" 中針	7.5 degrees W of N	Lai Wen-Chiun	twelfth century
(Outer) Heaven Plate	*Feng Chen—* "Seam Needle" 縫針	7.5 degrees E of N	Yang Yun-Sung	ninth century
Uneven divisions Table of 365.25 days or 360 degrees			Jesuit influence	sixteenth century
Hsiu				Ancient

Reasons for the Three Plates

Before explaining the real reason behind the three Plates, let us look at some of the hypotheses that have been put forward to explain this triplication of Plates. De Groot (1897, vol. 3:967) suggests that the other Plates were instituted to "improve accuracy of measurement." This contention can be easily dismissed by simply applying a protractor to any *lo p'an,* which will demonstrate that the sector measured by the "Correct Needle" of 360/24=15 degrees is widened to a possible 30 degrees by the addition of the other two Plates. Hence, accuracy is actually diminished not increased.

Needham (1962, vol. 4:299) was of the opinion that each of these Plates was introduced in response to changes to declination over time and produces figures in an attempt to corroborate this. However, his figures (1962, vol. 4:310) are of varying reliability and are taken geographically from all over China, where the declination would vary considerably anyway, even if all readings were taken in the same year, which they were not.

I think it unlikely that with widely fluctuating declinations both over time and in space, not to mention outcrops of rocks that produce wide local magnetic fluctuation, two sages should have hit upon the idea of creating new Plates exactly 7.5 degrees out of step with the original configuration, especially as at the time Yang Yun Sung proposed the "Seam Needle" variation of 7.5 degrees E of N, the actual observed declination was almost twice this. Besides, the idea of a fluctuation of declination over time was only consciously formulated during the Ming Dynasty over 800 years after Yang Yun Sung's time.

However, a passage from Wu T'ien Hung's *Lo Ching Chih Nan P'o Wu Chi* ("A South-pointer to Disperse the Fog about the *Lo p'an*"), dating from the sixteenth century, throws an unexpected light on the problem:

> Master Ch'iu (Yen-Han) got [his knowledge of the *Cheng Chen* from] Thai i Lao Jen . . . (but) there is also a "Heaven-measurement" (*t'ien chi*) and an "Earth-record" (*ti chi*). The *Fen-chin* divisions are arranged in three [Rings] . . .

This establishes the three Plates. He goes on (without a break) to point out a slight drawback and its solution:

> so that although for the earth [Plate] one follows the Cheng Chen ("Correct Needle") as everyone knows . . . in the north [the needle] declined to the NE, and in the south it declined to the SW. . .

This is a tricky passage. It either means that in Northern China the needle tended to decline to the NE or that, examining the northern side of the compass, he became aware of a NE declinational error. Whichever it is, the solution of adding two extra deflected scales was proposed.

> Therefore Master Yang [Yun-Sung] added the *Feng Chen* ("Seam Needle"). But in the "Heaven-measurement,"

the needle in the north is declined to the NW, and in the south it declined to the SE. Therefore Master Lai (Wen-Chun) added the *Chung Chen* ("Central Needle").

Wu T'ien Hung in this passage confirms the authorship of the two later Plates, which is useful, but still seems to suggest that the other Plates were simply a response to a difference of declination. I believe that this is not the correct reason for the existence of these extra Plates.

It is not coincidental that both Plates should vary exactly 7.5 degrees from the original "Correct Needle" because 7.5 degrees is exactly half of one of the twenty-four Mountains that form the basis of the Ring system. Wu T'ien-Hung says that "for Earth one follows the Cheng Chen ('Correct Needle') as everyone knows," implying that the Inner Ring was commonly used to determine the Earth directions, while the other Rings are for other more specialized applications.

In fact, the three Plates reflect the Chinese insistence on the interaction of the three levels of Earth, Man, and Heaven, where the main divisions of each Ring are reflected in each of these planes. The effect each has upon the other is the basic rationale of feng shui, which hopes to divine the parallels, and allow man to effect changes in both Heaven and Earth, and in their combined influence upon himself.

Each of these Rings in fact has a different function. The inner Ring, whose alignment is that of the Correct Needle to magnetic north/south, is used solely in conjunction with the alignment of the site—Earth. The middle region of the *lo p'an* disc, the Man Plate, measures surrounding man-made landform features, like other buildings, towers, walls, and so on. The outer region of the *lo p'an* disc, the Heaven Plate, measures water flows. These usages are an established part of San He feng shui practice. This means that there is not just a declinational difference or even a "theological" difference between the Plates, but each Plate is specifically used for a different purpose. This is something that either Wu T'ien-Hung did not know, or was not letting on.

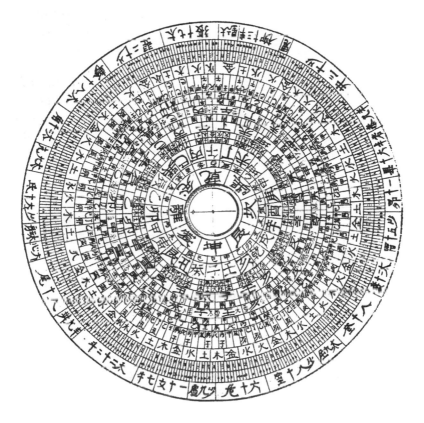

Figure 19. Analysis of the rings of a full lo p'an

Lo p'an *Size*

The average *lo p'an* (especially Mixed *lo p'ans* with both San He and San Yuan formulas) has more like sixteen to twenty Rings, considerably less than the full prescriptive thirty-eight of the *Lo Ching Chieh.*

On better made *lo p'ans* there may be a Ring subdivision of the 360 degrees of the circle also included on the "Central Needle." This, because of its Jesuit origins, is a sufficient hint of the relative modernity of the "Central Needle." However, because of the sheer physical difficulty of subdividing the Ring into 360 sectors, it is more usual for that Ring to be moved out beyond the Plate system to the outermost Ring along with the unevenly divided *hsiu* in the penultimate position. The lo p'an in Figure 19, examined by De Groot in the late nineteenth century, despite showing many rings, does not have one of 360 degrees. Instead the *hsiu* is the outer Ring, and the penultimate ring is the *hsiu* measuring scale divided into 365.25 "daily" degrees, linking the daily passage of the moon with its twenty-eight Mansions.

6

Making the *Lo p'an* Work

The sun has gone through its degrees, the moon through its conjunctions, the stars returned to their Stems, the year will soon begin again.

—*Li Chi* ("Book of Rites")

The *lo p'an* is used by the feng shui practitioner to take bearings on the points where various landscape formations, dragons, or rivers appear to terminate, disappear, enter or leave the landscape, from the point of view of the site where the reading is taken.

The needle is first aligned with the red hairline drawn on the bottom of the needle well. Then make sure that the trigrams in Ring 2 are located in their correct quarters. For example the Ch'ien trigram should be located in the south (using the Former Heaven Sequence of the inner ring) which should approximate the red pointed end of the needle.

Each limb of the dragon, knob, promontory, pool, watercourse, or man made object has its bearings taken, often using a red thread with two weights on it which is draped over the *lo p'an*, passing through its center, and aligned with the object being sighted. The various segments of the *lo p'an* that the thread crosses indicates the nature of the connection between the site under consideration and the feature whose bearing is being taken. Such "bearings" are taken of every significant landform feature visible from the building site or *hsueh*.

Thus the direction of the dragon veins, especially where they come to a head, which may be a cliff or the end of a line of hills, the position of pools or lines of drainage levees, intersection of rivers (even paths, railroad tracks, and existing architectural lines) must be taken into account, as each may carry some part of the flow of *ch'i* through the landscape. On flat land, woods, boulders, or large trees may mark the passage of *ch'i* through the Earth, although these areas do not have the vigor of mountains or sloped sites, which have more of the primal yang energy of the *ch'i*. Wells and springs, as they may be the "eyes and ears" of the dragon, are especially important features.

Ch'i, being the life-blood of the living earth, and indirectly of the creatures crawling upon its body, fluctuates in much the same way as the pulses of the human body. Traditional Chinese medicine has always been much concerned with the measurement of various pulses at different points in the anatomy, drawing deductions about the state of health from the differences between each pulse rate. It is a natural extension, therefore, to expect that the health of the earth can be determined by checking the pulse or cyclical phase of the *ch'i*.

Where there is "ceasing *ch'i*," the way is left open for incursions of *sha*. Traditionally, half the *lo p'an* contains directions that are prone to the ingress of *sha*, although this does not mean that *sha* will necessarily be generated at these points, merely that a weakness is implied.

Obviously, especially in a city or suburban feng shui reading, the features that are going to impinge on the site are road alignments, trees, and adjoining high buildings. Factors such as the line taken by adjoining rooftops or the *lo p'an* reading for any break or notch in the skyline should also be noted.

At a very basic level, any suspected unfavorable direction can be diagnosed by examining the mutual destruction order of the five Elements (see Chapter 4). Thus a feature that might be classified under the Element Metal because of its shape will cause "wasting away and injury" if placed in a Wood direction because "Metal destroys Wood." Thus "Metal destroying Wood" means wasting away, and "Earth destroying Water" might indicate illness. "Water destroying Fire" might mean death in youth, while "Fire destroying Metal" predisposes a site to natural calamities. Other calamities such as loss of office or lack of offspring may also be indicated. These Elemental directions can be read from the *lo p'an*.

When using the *lo p'an* indoors for the determination of the feng shui qualities of a room or building, the square base is placed parallel to the door or wall in question. Two pieces of red thread or nylon stretched at right angles across the disc bisect the disc into four quarters. These two threads parallel the orientation of the building, while the disc of the *lo p'an* is rotated until the south-pointing needle coincides with the red marking in the "Heaven Pool" or needle well under the glass. Make sure the sharp end points south (toward *wu*, 午) and the bulbous end aligns with the two dots on the floor of the needle well.

The practitioner then ascertains where the red threads cut the disc at both the facing and sitting directions and reads off the bearings from this. The practitioner might choose to use one of the three plates, Earth Plate, Man Plate, or Heaven Plate, depending upon his purposes, and reads off the precise bearing in terms of the twenty-four Mountains. For greater insight into the exact qualities of each direction, he could read the subdivisions of the twenty-four Mountains into sixty Dragons, seventy-two Dragons, or even 120 *fen-chin*.

When it is decided which of the surrounding features or veins of *ch'i* is the most auspicious, a sighting is taken of it and its sexagenary character is determined. From that the six days (1/60th) of the year appropriate to the character are determined. Now if the burial or building takes place within these six days, thenceforth the site is forever connected with this source of *ch'i*.

It is rather like a turnstile that revolves one complete turn per year with an entrance that is open for six days to each of the sixty directions at any time and the influence of the *ch'i* from that point. If the burial takes place at the time of the appropriate source of *ch'i*, this source of *ch'i* will continue to serve the grave or building for the whole of the year, not just six days a year, to the partial exclusion of all the other sources of *ch'i* or *sha*, good, bad, or indifferent.

It is as if the opening of the grave, or in the case of a house, the settling of the roof beams, opens a specific *ch'i* vein that remains attached to and feeds the site from then on. It is easy to see how important it is to "pounce" on the right time of the year to get access to the best *ch'i* vein the site has to offer.

If further accuracy is required, Ring 25 of the *lo p'an* of Wu Wang Kang breaks down each sexagenary character into six sections, being the lines of its hexagram, enabling accuracy to be increased to a one-day period. Modern *lo p'ans* tend to show the full sixty-four hexagrams on their San Yuan rings, but nineteenth-century *lo p'ans* sometimes omitted the four cardinal hexagrams in order to better fit the sixty remaining hexagrams to the numerical symbolism of the rest of the Plate.

If one wishes to improve the existing feng shui influences of a place, then this technique can be used to "open" a new vein of beneficial *ch'i* by altering the flow of *ch'i* during the six chosen days.

Besides the use of the *lo p'an* to determine the correct day or six-day period, there is also a need to apply data from the horoscope of the owner of the building with the recommendations of the current year's *Tung Sing*, or Chinese Almanac, observed together for that particular day, month, and year. The birth date of the owner should not, for example, clash with the date indicated by the sexagenary character allotted to the *ch'i* vein with which it is proposed to connect the site.

It is necessary for the sexagenary character of an owner's birth year to coincide with those of the site, but it is not so dangerous if the sexagenary characters of the month, day, or hour clash with those of the site. Until the birth year at least coincides, building or alteration to an existing feng shui configuration should be postponed.

The initial complexity of the *lo p'an* is due to the fact that the *lo p'an* bears in "fossilized form" on its face practically every system of time or space enumeration of any importance at any time in China. Consequently some of the older rings are at variance with the newer ones. A good example is the ring of 365.25 days not quite measuring the same thing as the ring of 360 degrees, a concept that was introduced in the sixteenth century into China by the Jesuits, who convinced the emperor that their astronomy was right by successfully predicting an eclipse.

Household
Feng Shui

7
Traditional House Structure

Feng shui not only applies to the landscape and town planning but also to houses and even specific rooms. The redecoration of a room or the reorienting of the furniture, particularly a bed, does not have as great an effect as changing the external feng shui, but it can still have a greater effect on the occupants than might be expected. It can not only change their sleep patterns at a physical level, but it can also change their luck, in other words, the quality of their relationship with the events and people in their lives.

Feng shui *hsien-sheng* are trained to see the changing patterns of the landscape and to use the *lo p'an* to diagnose the reason for prevailing good or bad influences, and their likely effects on any particular man-made or natural structure. The same applies inside the home or office where the interior "landscape" effects the people who live and work there. To understand many of the rules of household feng shui it is necessary to have a rough idea of the design of a traditional Chinese house, so that you can appreciate how they were derived.

Like the body, every house has orifices, doors, and windows that need to take in the flow of *ch'i* that must then circulate without stagnating to enable the house to "breathe." No room should be blocked off or difficult to navigate because it is too full of awkward furniture. These openings must be well guarded against the direct ingress of any "secret arrows" generated by the alignment of adjoining buildings or streets.

Typical traditional Chinese houses consist of one- or two-storied structures arranged around a central courtyard. The more ambitious households sometimes have two or more adjoining courtyards. Most are made of brick and stone with white or yellow lime plaster and with tiled roofs and floors made of wood or brick.

More complicated houses sometimes have a series of three interconnecting doors that alternately enter from the street, from the east, south and east as the guest comes through to the central courtyard, proceeding in each direction in turn. The doors and screen often have elaborately hand-carved woodwork and are surmounted by decorative and protective lintels, sometimes with a wooden structure or a sort of tiled cover with winglike projections similar to the roof of a mini-pagoda. Quite often a wall, unbreached by windows, surrounds the entire house so that only one main entrance is apparent, and this is often flanked or blocked by a "shadow wall" that prevents the direct access in a straight line of any *sha* or evil influence.

As a rule there are three rooms on each side of the four sides enclosing a courtyard, which is usually paved with

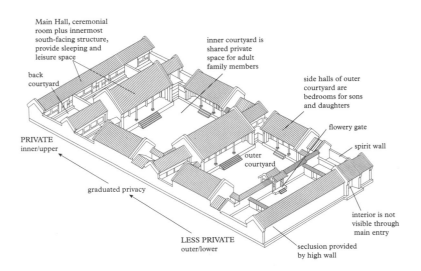

Main Hall, ceremonial room plus innermost south-facing structure, provide sleeping and leisure space

back courtyard

inner courtyard is shared private space for adult family members

side halls of outer courtyard are bedrooms for sons and daughters

flowery gate

spirit wall

PRIVATE inner/upper

outer courtyard

graduated privacy

interior is not visible through main entry

LESS PRIVATE outer/lower

seclusion provided by high wall

Figure 20. Typical Chinese house plan

stone slabs. Ground-floor rooms on each side are usually a reception or living room, with two flanking rooms often being used as bedrooms. At each corner, with a small opening onto the courtyard, are the kitchen or service rooms carefully tucked away so as not to be too obvious. A covered walkway at this level typically provides veranda space around the perimeter of the courtyard.

On the second floor level, the most important room is the ancestral shrine which traditionally takes the central room on the north or west side, while the rest of the rooms are often storerooms or subsidiary bedrooms. The ancestral shrine receives a daily offering of incense and maybe one or two dishes of simple food, with more elaborate celebrations on the fifteenth day of the seventh lunar month and various other festivals of the ancestors throughout the year.

The feng shui aspects of the lower floor are carefully considered in allocating the bedrooms for the various members of the extended family, the best going to the most important member of the family. Best, however, does not always mean the most attractive room for living in, but the most auspicious from the point of feng shui orientation. Conformity to traditional house design is to a large degree a symptom of competition for family superiority, where the residences were not so much considered as places to house individual members in comfort and ease, but as signs of unity and social prestige for the family group as a whole, both the living and the dead.

A typical double courtyard household would have its main entrance from the south side, with the ancestral shrine and best bedrooms possibly located in the west and kitchen and service facilities at the rear corners. The rooms dividing the two courtyards are open in both directions to permit access through them, and a subsidiary door might open to the east. However there would seldom be a main entrance opening to the north, as this would permit the access of *sha* or the cold winds of the north—a practical consideration as well as a feng shui one. Such entrances have often been bricked up on the advice of a feng shui *hsien-sheng*.

Because of the idea of an extended family with room left for the developing lineage, Chinese houses are often too large for the people currently occupying them. It is the usual practice to build a basic courtyard and then fill in the rooms along each side starting in the north and the west, so that the house is well "backed," later adding a second courtyard or a second floor. Often the house's extension outstrips the growth of a prosperous family.

Quite often the rooms on the ground floor used most are, by Western standards, too dark because of the broad covered corridors extending in front of them. The internal courtyard itself with rooms on all sides gives little opportunity for the sun to enter a room because it is screened by the projecting veranda roofing, but in hot climates this can be useful. The covered corridors that extend around the house quite often on the southern side also help to promote the bad ventilation, although probably originally they were an insulation and a security measure.

Following the same theme, guests were often unable to enter the house directly, but had to skirt around a shadow wall designed to repel the direct approach of *sha* or *kuei* (demons or ghosts). The shadow wall is a separate segment of wall about as high as the others but standing alone and facing the main portal to the family home. Sometimes the family has two or three such walls, each facing one of the several portals, and on each of these is quite often inscribed four large characters "confirming" the good feng shui of the household and screening it from any damaging outside influences.

Maybe the architectural background to the shadow wall owes its origin to military strategic design, when the wall served to prevent a large number of armed men entering the household at any one time. Perhaps the practical exigency was generalized to the point where the protection became symbolically important as well.

Obviously poor homes have few of these complicated architectural features and depend largely upon written characters and hanging plaques to defend their doorways, which in the poorest case, lead directly into the family living room with a fully visible shrine, without benefit of any deflecting screen or wall.

Temple Feng Shui

Not only is a person's destiny and well-being affected by where he lives or where he buries his ancestors, but it is also affected by where he works and where he worships.

The home orientation rules can also be applied to public buildings, offices, and temples.

The correct feng shui location of temples was also of the utmost importance, not just for its finances, but also for the well-being of its worshipers. In Hong Kong alone, there were in excess of 600 temples, mostly Buddhist or Taoist, serving a population of what is now almost 7 million. Almost all of these would have been built with feng shui input, although some of that good feng shui has been subsequently destroyed by the growth of high-rise buildings around them. In Singapore, temples that once lined the shores of the sea are now miles inland due to land reclamation projects.

Obviously in such overcrowded areas the demands of modern life and building regulations have led to many temples being built in areas not considered completely auspicious from a feng shui point of view. To counteract this, *pa kua* mirrors are often seen in windows or doorways to reflect "secret arrows." Because of the maritime nature of Hong Kong, a number of temples are not located on the pulse of the dragon but "in front of a dragon stretching down from hill to sea." This means that these temples are situated between two spurs of a hill on a slope down to a valley or directly opening onto the sea. A particularly good example is Tin Hau's temple at Joss House Bay.

The traditional Chinese temple consists of three main halls, each leading into the others. At the front entrance is the bell tower where the temple's bell and drum should be kept. Behind this is the smoke tower, where Hell money and paper offerings are burned in huge urns, the smoke from which rises and escapes through an opening in the roof of a tower formed by pillars elevating its roof above the other roofing. Directly behind this is the main hall or palace, with its altars to the principal gods, which will often be mixed Taoist and Buddhist. Many temples have side halls to accommodate the minor deities, usually attached to which are kitchens or quarters for the temple keeper and his family. At the back will often be found an ancestors' hall. This often has a series of racks, each corresponding to one generation, which bear plaques commemorating the ancestors from that generation. At the top and back will often be the original settlers who came to Hong Kong or Singapore in the nineteenth century.

The main altars themselves are effectively at the back of the temple with the entrance opening on to the auspicious south. The most modern temples seem to have dispensed with the bell tower and smoke tower, preferring a more practical external incinerator partly to eliminate the risk of fire and partly to reduce the smoke-blackening of the ceilings.

The roofs of the temples are their most ornate feature, as these are responsible for the interaction of the temple with the Elements and the wind. The ridges are richly decorated and encrusted with figures representing divinities, folk heroes, and even frogs and insects, often made of porcelain. The coloring is also symbolic: red for happiness; green for peace and eternity; white also for peace and occasionally for mourning; with gold for royalty, strength, and wealth. Earth colors also make their appearance. The predominance of gold and red in Chinese culture speaks for itself.

One of the most common roof symbols is of course the dragon that pursues the flaming pearl. The rippling carvings of dragons on the lines of the roof are designed to stimulate the flow of the dragon force, the *ch'i,* into the temple itself. Other temple animal symbolism includes the carp (with its ability to swim upstream against the flow of water, and eventually turn into a dragon), which may also be found live in pools in the temple grounds.

The other most important Chinese symbolic animal, the lion, portrayed in a highly stylized form (for it is some time since real lions were known in China), acts as a pair of temple door guardians. Lions were in fact introduced into China by Buddhists from India, and during their relatively brief appearance engendered many myths.

In office buildings, carvings of the sacred animals are used for much the same purposes, with lions particularly being used as portal guardians. The same stress that is laid upon color in the temples also applies to the home where ill-aspected rooms should be decorated with strong colors like red or gold on the carpets or tapestry, and perhaps the occasional black-painted door, with care to choose the right Element. Black is symbolic of Water (not blue as in the West). As Water is also associated with wealth, so black is frequently part of the color scheme.

Red is used as it is symbolic of happiness and prosperity, gold for its obvious symbolism, yellow for gaiety, and green for a quiet atmosphere. However, you should be careful that no red wall faces west or black one faces south, as black is the color of the north which must not be made to confront its opposite.

8

Simple House Rules

Feng shui has complex formulas, but it also has simple rules that every traditional Chinese family (or at least the older generation) knows and follows instinctively.

For example, a student not doing well in his studies might be advised to move his desk to another quarter or to face a different direction (in line with his birth year trigram or *kua* number), and the repositioning of a sickbed might well make the difference in enabling a patient to recover more rapidly. Nor is this just the stimulus of a new view, it is as basic as the orientation of a plant toward light or away from it, so a patient may flourish or fade according to his or her bed orientation. With correct feng shui orientation he or she can take advantage of positive, natural healing forces.

One of the classics of feng shui is the *Yang Chai*, or "Yang Dwelling Manual," dealing especially with the siting of houses (not graves, for yang dwellings are the houses of the living). The *Yang Chai* gives over a hundred diagrams with detailed text and commentary showing many different situations and combinations of architectural features including trees, roads, temples, graves, paths, and mounds. It is such texts that form the bulk of the feng shui currently available in English. The general rules applying to different situations are explained at the beginning of the book, while the whole of the last section deals with houses sited inauspiciously in relation to temples and monasteries and with those houses whose inhabitants' children have little success in school, examinations, or jobs.

The *Yang Chai* also recommends various talismans with instructions for their preparation, such as the kind of ink, size, and type of board to be used to neutralize or overcome certain situations or influences that could occur at particular times of the year. A typical talisman might be inscribed with the characters "T'ai-shan dares to resist (the evil influences)," thus invoking the might of China's most sacred mountain to fend off *sha* (noxious vapors) and *kuei* (鬼, ghosts or demons). Such a talisman is typically written in red by a Taoist priest on a peachwood board about fourteen inches in length. Its setting up might be accompanied by a sacrifice of food, drink, or incense. These talismans exist in the no-man's land between feng shui, magic, and Taoist religion and are an auxiliary technique designed to deal with some problems. Much of the talisman usage is common to general Taoist practice, and simple examples can be found in the Chinese almanacs that are published annually.

Figure 21. Drawings of talismans from the Tung Shu, *or Chinese Almanac*

In general terms the main orientation of a house might be southward, but more important the sitting position of the house (usually the opposite side to the main entrance) should be located on the owner's most auspicious direction (see Eight Mansion, Chapter 9). If there is no range of hills or supporting wall at the back of the site, then the planting of a row of trees on this side can be beneficial, as these will help "support" the house.

In southern China every house, hamlet, and village lacking the necessary hill configuration has a small grove of bamboo or trees behind it for this purpose and a pond in front. If possible, a pond with running water and a rather tortuous drainage system could be created in the same fashion, especially if the site is lucky enough to slope down toward the south. The laying out of water according to "Water Dragon" formulas is a topic too complex to be covered here, but is the subject of a forthcoming book by the present author.

The garden is of course that part of the landscape that is under your control and therefore offers an opportunity to enhance the feng shui. If your garden is laid out in a square fashion, maybe the introduction of a little imagination to give it more natural lines could work wonders. Specifically, a straight path from the street directly to the front door is undesirable: try re-laying it with gentle curves.

More technical operations could include deflecting *sha* alignments with a *pa kua* mirror, which can be cheaply bought in almost any big city Chinatown area. This is an octagonal board with the eight trigrams (in the Former Heaven Sequence) painted around a mirror, which faces the oncoming *sha* with a view to deflecting it. Alternatives to this are the positioning of stone lions or pottery dragons or even a tiger's head with a sword gripped in its fierce mouth at strategic positions. But as Eitel says, "by far the best and most effective means is to engage a geomancer [feng shui master], to do what he says, and to pay him well." One of the recurring problems that faces feng shui masters, especially in the West, is that, after receiving advice, the client then neglects to follow it, but still complains that the feng shui has not worked. The changes recommended need to be done properly, not half-heartedly, for the feng shui to work.

The bulk of the more than 600 titles printed on feng shui in English concentrate upon these simple devices and "cures" within and around the home, rather than taking into consideration the often more important surrounding landform features or the formulas inscribed on the *lo p'an*. Very few Westerners involve themselves with the far more demanding principles and practices of Compass School feng shui, preferring to stick to simple, and sometimes superstitious, rules of thumb.

Many modern Chinese texts on feng shui are also concerned with urban feng shui: the location of houses and the orientation of their rooms and doors. A number of popular texts written along these lines circulate in Malaysia, Singapore, Hong Kong, and Taiwan. A selection of rules to be observed in the construction or purchase of a house (almost a house buyer's guide to feng shui) could be excerpted from such manuals, and two such guides are listed in the bibliography.

Some rules can seem like common sense. To build or buy a house that has a large tree directly in front of the doorway is not only inconvenient but considered to be overpoweringly bad feng shui, as it deflects the "entry of wealth." It is also considered inauspicious to build or buy a house situated on a triangular or oddly shaped piece of land: regular and rectangular is better. If the house is lucky enough to have a traditional central courtyard, then one should be careful not to have a tree or pond located at the exact center of the courtyard because that also detracts from the *ch'i* accumulation of the house itself.

The arrangement of the rooms and facilities within the house is not only traditional but hedged around with a number of taboos. The most obvious stipulation is that the primary rooms that are used most often should, like the house, face the south.

General rules have become common, but in many cases these are just the result of a popular writer mistakenly

。處心中宅住於置配宜，間房的人主

A

下地，房住築建地林樹在
。根發的樹有留要不

C

。面東南在設宜房人老

B

Figure 22. Simple household feng shui rules

An example of simple rule-of-thumb feng shui. The Chinese captions read:

A: The master bedroom should be located in the center of the house.

B: The family's eldest members' bedroom should be located facing the southeast.

C: If building a house in a forest, be sure that there is no decayed tree stump lurking under the soil.

universalizing a specific example, and each case should be examined on its own merits. Examples of such overgeneralization include, "if the premises is to be used as a shop, it should be certain not to face either the northeast or southwest." If a residential property, the kitchen should preferentially face east, and certainly not northwest, which is the most inauspicious location for a kitchen (because NW is the location of the Heaven trigram Ch'ien in the Later Heaven Sequence and having the fire of the kitchen burning there is akin to laying "fire at Heaven's Gate").

The eldest members of the family should, if possible, have rooms facing the southeast, not in the primary direction of the south (or the front of the house), which should be allocated to the current head of the family. Sometimes it is suggested that elderly members of the family take rooms facing the west.

Obviously practical suggestions, such as that a house without a rear door is dangerous, although subsumed under the heading of feng shui, seem to be more in the province of common sense. Other regulations would delight the heart of a health inspector in any country, for it is suggested that a bedroom should not open directly onto a kitchen, and that a toilet should not face directly onto the main entrance of the house.

A particularly Chinese restriction is that the family altar should not be observable from the street—not only does this lower respect for the family, but it also leaves the family tutelary god open to attack or ridicule from the public. Conversely, in many Chinese-owned shops the altar will be in full view of the street so that it can help to draw in customers from the street.

Constructional rules that are a combination of common structural good sense and feng shui rationale include stipulations that one should not build on top of a buried well. This applies for several reasons. First the well is yin, and that will cause the house to be yin. Second, from a feng shui point of view, to fill up wells in order to build one's house is the equivalent of closing the breathing orifices of the dragon, and this it is supposed may in turn promote sickness of the eyes or ears of those living in the house.

Similarly, it is advised that one should not construct, renovate, or reconstruct a house in which one of the family members is pregnant, as the forces of the cosmos are considered to be adequate only for the bringing to birth of one child, or one house, at a time.

If you survey the site before building, then be sure that there is no decayed tree stump lurking under the soil, for this is an extremely inauspicious feng shui indication that will blight any house built above or near it. The theory is that the thwarted growth of the tree will take out its frustration on the newly "grown" house by blighting its occupants (see Figure 22).

In terms of construction materials, it is considered to be not only aesthetically unpleasant but also inauspicious to use timber as vertical beams if they are stood in the reverse direction to that in which they grew during their lives as trees. If the grain of the wood and the natural direction of growth point upward, then those in the household will increase in prosperity rather than the opposite.

There is much talk about the relationship between facilities in a house in such manuals, and most of the suggestions are counsels of perfection in terms of the allocation of living space, but have their roots in common sense. It is, for example, bad feng shui to connect either two bedrooms (with a loss of independence for both occupants) or two bathrooms. Bedrooms should never be built over either empty spaces, garages, or empty storerooms as this creates a *ch'i* vacuum underneath and affects the occupants adversely, leaving them without support.

The gateway of the house should, by the same rule, not be bigger than the entranceway to the house, for it thereby detracts from the *ch'i* accumulation of the household. There should be ample room in front of any garage entrance.

In the kitchen are rules that equate water with yin and fire with yang, and that suggest that they do not confront each other, so that a sink or a refrigerator (Water) should not confront a stove (Fire). Yang should in each case slightly predominate over yin to obtain a favorable feng shui balance.

The setting up of furniture in a way that does not obstruct the smooth flow of *ch'i* from room to room is also an important consideration. Each window and door should be considered from the point of view of the inflowing *ch'i*, which should be led by the general lines of the furnishings in a curved path from room to room before it exhausts itself. No room should be cut off from the rest of the house in such a way that it can become a repository for stagnant *ch'i*, unless it is a room containing bad "stars" that needs to be left quiet to prevent activating these. The converse of this is true: that a room with too many doors is not only drafty in the physical sense but is liable to be a disperser of *ch'i*. Consideration should be given to sealing up one or two of the doors to such a room. It should also be easy to move from room to room without bumping into the corners of protruding furnishings, for the flow of *ch'i* is very much like the movements of a dancer who will not perform well on a cluttered stage.

There are a number of key points in the architecture of the traditional house that need to be considered from a feng shui point of view. These "dwelling elements" include:

1. The Gate and Main Entrance Door
2. The Courtyard
3. Cooking Stove
4. Toilet

Let's look at these elements one at a time.

The Gate and Main Entrance Door

All classical feng shui texts emphasize that the gate [or main door] of a building is the mouth of the house through which flows the main auspicious *ch'i* entering the building. Of all the feng shui points of interest in a building, the gate or door is therefore perhaps the most important. The Chinese character *men* (門) can refer to either the gate or the front door of a building. Gates of course are more likely to be found in rural areas, and city dwellers mostly do without the luxury of a separate gate. The gate and the door can however face quite different directions, and this raises questions as to which should be used. To decide this, it is very useful to go back to the original rules of feng shui to see how these two things interrelate.

Nowadays the question is more often raised as to which facing direction should be taken in an apartment block: that of the street door to the whole block, or the apartment door onto the corridor on the apartment's own floor. If you interpret this in terms of first principles, then you can easily see that the whole block doorway and facing direction correspond to the main gate, or *ta men* (with its access to a compound that may contain many buildings, but whose feng shui is governed by the facing direction of this gate). The individual apartment door or entrance to the main house in a compound corresponds with the lesser *chung-men*, and the *tsung-men* is the door which actually opens on to the main living room. In small apartments the last two are often the same. Lastly the *pien men* is the door to the utility part of the house, such as the kitchen or laundry door. At individual room level each door is referred to as the *fang men*.

There are detailed rules governing all these doors, but let us return to the question of apartment blocks. The *Pa Chai Ming Ching* ("Eight Mansion Ming Classic") states that the *ta men* "is the most important one. It must be open to the most auspicious direction of the main house building." This resolves the apparent problem. It is therefore the apartment block door that conditions the qualities of the incoming *ch'i*, not the door to the individual apartment.

Obviously the direction in which the gate/main door faces determines the overall benefit or otherwise for the occupants. This will be examined in more depth in the Eight Mansion chapter.

The Courtyard

The interior courtyard is not often a feature of modern homes, but it was important in classical feng shui as Chinese traditional houses, except the most rudimentary, had one or more courtyards. The courtyard provides practical functions like admitting light and air to the surrounding rooms, but more important, like the *ming t'ang* it helped to accumulate beneficial *ch'i*. In this context the treatment of water is very important, especially as the surrounding roofs will all drain into the courtyard, which will often have a pool. The drainage from this pool will follow the most contorted path possible before finally leaving the house. This is because water carries *ch'i* and therefore it was considered beneficial that water be retained as long as possible before finally being discharged.

There were various rules against having trees in the courtyard, primarily because they introduced too much yin, increased the humidity, and, if they grew too big, might dominate the house. Certainly they should not be planted in the center of the courtyard, in the Heavenly Heart, as this location was called.

Cooking Stove

The cooking stove is very important from a feng shui perspective for several reasons. The most often quoted is that it is responsible for preparing the family's food, and therefore their health and energy. This is true, but there is a more significant point and that concerns the Elemental energies.

If you think about it, Wood, Metal, and Earth are all static Elements, while Water and Fire can and do move. We saw how important physical water is to the feng shui of a building —its location, direction of flow, and so on. The other dynamic Element is of course Fire, and in the average house, the kitchen stove is the only real example of Fire. I am not talking here about the less important symbolic fire of red walls and furnishing, but the Element itself. These days, electricity has in many cases replaced wood, coal, coke, or gas as the heat source. My opinion is that electricity per se is not very Fiery, although its effects (heat and light) are definitely yang. A lot of modern feng shui practitioners go into detail about the direction of the electrical plug socket, and so on (as the source of Fire), but I do not think this is a valid extension of the traditional feng shui rules. The cooking stove must have a "fire-mouth" from which real heat (and preferably real fire) emerges to qualify for these rules.

In general the stove should be located on an unfavorable location in the kitchen. An unfavorable location is defined by the house's *kua* number.

The stove's fire-mouth or fuel-hole should face a beneficial direction, as defined by the occupant's *kua* number. By the occupant I mean the head of the household. By the *kua* number I mean this person's year of birth interpreted as a trigram. This trigram then gives their personal best directions. This means in broad terms that if the head of the household is a "West Group" person, then acceptable fire-mouth directions are W, NW, SW, and NE. If he or she is an "East Group" person, then acceptable fire-mouth pointing directions are N, S, E, and SE. We will look at how this is derived and the significance of the West/East Group division in Chapter 9 on the Eight Mansion formula.

There are also detailed rules about the *location* of the cooking stove using the twenty-four Mountain Ring of the *lo p'an*. Typically Water (north) and Metal (west) directions like *tzu, kuei,* or *ch'ien* are unfavorable because of the Element clash. The *Ch'ien* Mountain is the absolutely worst location for the stove (because of the "fire at Heaven's Gate" mentioned earlier). The best locations are in general terms the *yin, shen, chen, mao, ssu, ping,* and *keng* Mountains. Location of the stove in the *ken* and *yi* directions will tend to promote the likelihood of danger from physical fire, a danger much more real in traditional Chinese houses, but still relevant today.

The direction of the *pien men* (the side doorway to the kitchen) is also important and in a full analysis it interacts with the positioning of the cooking stove.

Toilet

In past times, the toilet was rightly considered a center of pestilence. Nowadays with modern sanitation its importance to feng shui has been played down. However, it is still one of the points of foul water evacuation in the house, and therefore must be an important feng shui consideration. As it is negative, it is ideal to place it in an inauspicious location, to suppress malignant *ch'i*. Obviously the toilet should not be located in the direction of *Ch'ien*, or Heaven's Gate. Apart from the considerations of a specific house, in general, directions such as Mountains *chia, ping, wu, hsin,* and *ch'ou* are considered okay, with *yin* and *kuei* (the Demon Gate) considered very favorable, as the toilet will then "press down" on that area. Strangely it is said that toilets located in *chen* and *hsun* will cause children to be disobedient and may cause loss of property. An interesting observation to look out for. Obviously the toilet must not face out the main door, or even a subsidiary door.

9

Roots of the Eight Mansion
Formula—*Pa chai*

There are many books that now explain the Eight Mansion formula in English, none of which existed when the present book first came out, so I do not intend to do anything more than recap lightly, and then point out some of the original Chinese source material upon which the modern explanations are based, in order to dispel a few misconceptions that have arisen by the continued rehashing of the formula without any reference back to original Chinese sources.

Briefly, both people and houses are classifiable by a trigram (or, if you prefer, "*kua* number"). This enables you to predict certain things first about the person (best work and sleep directions), second about the house, and third about the *interaction* of the person and the house. Obviously there can be $8 \times 8 = 64$ possible interactions between the person and the house. For those who get the hint, this actually leads to several other interesting formulas, related to the hexagrams of the *I Ching*, that are beyond the intended scope of this book.

1. A person's *kua* number is determined by his or her year of birth. The reason for this is that the trigram (in the case of a male) is in fact the trigram corresponding to the Annual Flying Star in the year he was born. This helps also to explain why for this calculation the 4th/5th of February is key, as this is the Annual Flying Star "changeover" date.

Be careful to deduct one from the year of birth if you were born between January 1 and February 4/5, to allow for the

Chinese solar year starting on February 4/5 rather than January 1. Do not use the Chinese lunar New Year calendar either, as many have suggested, because the lunar New Year does not relate to the Annual Flying Star.

The actual calculations are explained in many modern feng shui books, but in brief, add up all the digits of the year in which you were born, then if the answer is greater than 9, continue to add together its digits. If you are male, subtract the resulting number from 11, but if you are female add the number to 4. The result is your *kua* or trigram number. Two quick examples will suffice:

A male born in 1960
1+9+6+0 = 16 = 1+6 = 7
has a *kua* number of 11-7 = 4

A female born in 1960
1+9+6+0 = 16 = 1+6 = 7
has a *kua* number of 4+7 = 11 = 1+1 = 2

Incidentally, those who are familiar with this calculation may remark that the numbers 10 and 5 are more usually associated with the calculation, not 11 and 4. The results are the same, but this formula works also in the twenty-first century, while the more popular one did not. The final result will always be one of the 8 trigrams (numbers 1, 2, 3, 4, 6, 7, 8 or 9). In Table 17 I have also listed results for 5 (male) and 5 (female), but classically a trigram number of 5 will always be replaced by 8 (for a female) or 2 (for a male), because 5 is the number at the center, not one of the trigrams.

First result of the Eight Mansion formula. Once you have the personal *kua* number, you can consult Table 18 to see what the person's best directions are. You can see that four directions are listed as good and four as bad. The four best can be used to determine the best direction for a person to face when working or sleeping, *irrespective of the house* they are in. Typically facing your *sheng ch'i* while working, or sleeping with your head toward your *fu wei* is beneficial.

2. A house's *kua* number is determined by its sitting location. Mostly the sitting position will be directly opposite the facing direction or front door, but not always. Exceptions are explained in my *Flying Star Feng Shui*. The translation of sitting position into *kua* number is very simple:

Sitting Position	Trigram	House *kua* number	Group
N	K'an	1	East House
NE	Ken	8	West House
E	Chen	3	East House
SE	Hsun	4	East House
S	Li	9	East House
SW	K'un	2	West House
W	Tui	7	West House
NW	Ch'ien	6	West House

Incidentally, the formula is called *pa chai*, or Eight Mansion, because this calculation yields eight different types of house. Check the *kua* number of your house.

Second result of the Eight Mansion formula. With this knowledge you can decide which of the eight types of house is best for you, and so limit the selection if you are buying a new house to a house drawn from your own Group, be it West Group or East Group.

There has been some controversy in English texts as to whether the determination of House trigram is based on the sitting or facing direction of the house. I can say categorically that in all serious Chinese texts, the Palace that determines the trigram of a house is always its sitting location. Having said that, the concept of the "sitting side" of a house does not come naturally to an English reader, so some modern writers have used instead the facing direction of the house, but for that to be rightly applied, the rules have to be reversed, and this is not always done correctly.

Let us demonstrate this at its simplest level. If you are standing at the back of the house in the Sitting Palace, as you look forward out through the main door, then the Azure

Dragon is on your left and the White Tiger on your right. However, if you are on the facing side of the house, looking in through the front door, then the reverse is true. Basically to avoid all such problems it is better to always work from the Sitting Palace, even with formulas that are more complex than Eight Mansion.

3. One basic test of the feng shui compatibility of a person and a particular house is determined by the relationship between the house's *kua* number and the person's *kua* number.

This is the main part of the Eight Mansion formula. The three auspicious directions are *yen-nian* (lengthening of years), *t'ien-yi* (heavenly doctor), and *sheng-ch'i* (birth energy). English texts often include *fu wei*, but traditionally this was accorded a neutral status.

The classic text the *Yang Chai Ts'o Yao* states that:

> In general, if the sitting location [of the house is] the three auspicious directions of *sheng-ch'i*, *t'ien-yi*, or *yen-nian* according to the time-fate [*kua* number] of the householder, then the auspicious *ch'i* will enter the house when . . . the occupants go out and come in.

This passage is interesting. First of all it emphasizes that the auspicious *ch'i* is brought in by the foot traffic of the occupants. A correctly oriented but unused door brings no benefit at all. Second this one sentence ties together the *kua* number of the house and the *kua* number of the occupant. This is in fact the core of the Eight Mansion formula. Let me restate it in a more modern way:

Determine the *kua* number of the individual. Look up his three most auspicious directions (from Table 17). If any of these coincide with the *kua* number (or sitting direction) of the house, then this is a beneficial house for this person.

Soon this rule was simplified by pointing out that personal *kua* numbers fell into two groups, those who beneficial directions *sheng-ch'i*, *t'ien-yi*, or *yen-nian* plus *fu wei* were W, SW, NW, and NE, and those whose beneficial directions were N,

Table 17. Eight Mansion formula

The four best and four worst compass directions for each kua number.
This can be applied to personal (birth year) kua, or to the location of a building. The compass points are house sitting positions.

Chinese Name	Literal Meaning	Influence	Kua numbers									
			1	2	3	4	5(M)	5(F)	6	7	8	9
Best Four Directions/Locations:												
生氣 Sheng ch'i	generating ch'i	Success & great prosperity; best	SE	NE	S	N	NE	SW	W	NW	SW	E
延年 Yen-nien	lengthening years	Longevity; good for relationships & family	S	NW	SE	E	NW	W	SW	NE	W	N
天醫 T'ien i/yi	Heavenly Doctor	Health & regeneration	E	W	N	S	W	NW	NE	SW	NW	SE
伏位 Fu wei	house sitting location*	Mild good fortune/stability	N	SW	E	SE	SW	NE	NW	W	NE	S
Worst Four Directions/Locations:												
禍害 Huo hai	accidents & mishaps	Mild bad luck/mild physical injury	W	E	SW	NW	E	S	SE	N	S	NE
五鬼 Wu kuei	five ghosts	Mischief & quarrels.' litigation	NE	SE	NW	SW	SE	N	E	S	N	W
六煞 Liu sha	six evils/evil spirits	Six setbacks	NW	S	NE	W	S	E	N	SE	E	SW
絕命 Chueh ming	severed fate	Total loss/end of life.; worst	SW	N	W	NE	N	SE	S	E	SE	NW
Element =			Wa	E	Wo	Wo	E	E	M	M	E	F
Trigram/kua =			Kan	K'un	Chen	Hsun			Ch'ien	Tui	Ken	Li

* Literally, bowing position before the throne, or ambush position.

S, E, and SE. They soon became known as West Group and East Group people, respectively. Likewise houses could also be categorized as West Group or East Group houses. The rule could then be restated as: West Group people should live in West Group houses, and East Group people should live in East Group houses for the best results. Obviously there are many other feng shui determinations that can be applied, but this is the basic Eight Mansion formula.

You can see how categorizing people by their group is a lot faster and easier than by their *kua* number, followed by working out the best directions. You can also begin to see how the Eight Mansion formula overlaps with Flying Star formula, because of course they are all part and parcel of the same feng shui.

So that is how the thinking on the Eight Mansion formula developed. Hopefully you will never again be confused as to whether to use sitting or facing directions in determining a house's *kua* number. I have tested the rule on a number of Chinese mansions built for Ch'ing Dynasty mandarins, and it is confirmed by such structures. I have always found that practice is more reliable than theory, and that if you don't want to experiment, then the safest way to test feng shui rules is by looking at the work of acknowledged masters who worked for rich and successful clients, those who hired the best Imperial feng shui masters, rather than by merely appealing to texts. After all, the proof of the pudding is in the eating, not in reading the recipe.

I will not be looking at Flying Star formulas in this book as they are covered thoroughly by my book on *Flying Star Feng Shui*.* Aside from these two formulas, which have been popularized in the West, there are a host of other feng shui formulas equally as useful. Some of these will be detailed in my forthcoming book *Guide to the Feng Shui Compass*.†

---

* Tuttle Publishing, Rutland, Vermont, 2003.
† Golden Hoard Press, Singapore and London, 2007.

Feng Shui Glossary

The terms in this book are rendered in Wade-Giles transliteration. To help readers more familiar with *pinyin* transliteration, some of the *pinyin* equivalents have been cross-referenced in this glossary.

Almanac, Chinese: an annual Chinese publication that includes all kinds of advice, including Flying Star locations for the year and the best/worst activities for every day of the year.

Ba Zi: see *pa tzu.*

Bagua: see *pa kua.*

Bazhai: see *pa chai.*

Bird, Red: a Form School hill formation at the front of a house or site.

Book of Changes: see *I Ching.*

Branches: see Earthly Branches.

Bright Hall: see *ming t'ang.*

Calendar, lunar: a calendar based on the "months" measured by Moon cycles.

Calendar, solar: a calendar, like the standard Western one, based on the Earth's revolution around the sun, but more precisely aligned to the seasons.

Cardinal points: north, south, east, and west.

Celestial Animals: Azure Dragon, White Tiger, Black Tortoise with Snake (or Dark Warrior), and Red Bird.

Central Needle: the Man Plate reading of the second Ring of twenty-four Mountains. It deals with the measurement of surrounding "sand" or small landscape features and man-made buildings, fences, and so on.

Chai: house.

Chen: trigram of thunder and spring.

Cheng Chen: see Correct Needle.

Ch'ien trigram: the trigram of Heaven and late autumn.

Ch'i: the vital energy of the universe, in man, the heavens, and earth, sometimes referred to as "cosmic breath."

Chin Dynasty: 221–206 BC.

Ch'ing Dynasty: 1644–1911 AD.

Chor sin: (Cantonese) see Mountain Star.

Chou Dynasty: 1027–221 BC.

Chueh ming: severed fate or total loss of life location in house.

Chung Chen: see Central Needle.

Compass, Chinese: see *lo p'an.*

Compass School: the Fukien [Fujian] School of feng shui that uses the *lo p'an* to locate and diagnose *ch'i* flows. More correctly called the *Fang Wei* (Directions and Positions) School.

Correct Needle: The Earth Plate reading of the inner Ring of twenty-four Mountains.

Daoism: see Taoism.

Destructive Cycle: the cycle of the Elements that is ordered: Metal, Wood, Earth, Water, Fire.

Direction: one of the eight main compass points, or in a more specialized sense, the twenty-four Mountain ring on the *lo p'an.*

Dragon, Azure: the Form School hills to the left of a house or site (looking out from the front door). The Chinese word *ching,* which means both green and blue, is used to describe this dragon and therefore the translation compromise of "azure" has been used.

Dragon Gate: the gate through which successful scholars are supposed to pass, metaphorically turning from a carp into a dragon.

Dragon, Green: see Dragon, Azure.

Dragon, Yellow: the Celestial Animal associated with the Central Palace.

Earth Base: When a house is built it is thought that the act of building encapsulates the Earth energies of that Period or Time into the structure. This Period number is the Earth Base.

Earthly Branches: (*ti shih*) the twelve divisions of the day, or the year, which are combined with the ten Heavenly Stems to form the sixty sexagenary characters.

East Group: people or houses whose best locations are SE, N, S, and E.

East/West system: the system that divides people and houses into two types, the East Group and the West Group.

Eight Mansion formula: the feng shui division of a room or building into eight sectors, whose qualities vary according to the facing/sitting direction of the house. A subset of Eight Mansion theory (popularized by Lillian Too) attributes aspirations to specific directions, such as Career, Wealth, Marriage, and so on.

Elements, five: the *wu hsing*—Water, Fire, Earth, Metal, and Wood.

Facing direction: The front side of building, often, but not always, the side on which is located the front door.

Facing Star: see Water Star

Fang wei: see Compass School.

Fei hsing: see Flying Stars.

Fei sin: see Flying Stars.

Feng: wind.

Feng chen: see Seam Needle.

Feng sha: a noxious, *ch'i*-destroying wind.

Feng shui: the Chinese system of maximizing the accumulation of beneficial *ch'i* to improve the quality of life and luck of the occupants of a particular building or location. Literally "wind water."

Flying Stars: a system of feng shui that relates the changes in the qualities of particular sectors of a building to the periodic and annual movements of differing types of *ch'i* related to the nine stars of the Big Dipper/Northern Ladle constellation.

Form and Configuration School: *hsing shih*, feng shui practice that uses landform structure to determine positions of maximum beneficial *ch'i* accumulation. Its most famous master was Yang Yun Sung (840–c.888 AD).

Former Heaven Sequence: or *hou t'ien*, a circular arrangement of the eight trigrams, such that the trigram Ch'ien is in the south. Used on defensive *pa kua* mirrors, and for the feng shui of exterior landforms.

Four Pillars: your personal Chinese horoscope, specifically the eight Chinese characters and their associated Elements generated by determining the Stem and Branch of each of the year, month, day, and hour of a birth date.

Fu-Hsi: an early ruler of China said to have discovered or invented the trigrams.

Fu wei: house location that has mild good fortune.

Fu Xi: see *Fu-Hsi.*

Ganzhi system: see *kan shih* system.

Geomancy: an old *mis*-translation of "feng shui." In reality geomancy is a completely different Arab system of divination by dots and sand originating in North Africa in the ninth century AD.

Great Cycle of 180 years: nine cycles of twenty years. The current Great Cycle began in 1864.

Green Dragon: see Dragon, Azure.

Han Dynasty: 202 BC–220 AD.

Heavenly Stems (*t'ien kan*): the ten characters that represent the cycle of the five Elements in both their yin and yang form. They combine with the twelve Earthly Branches to form the sixty sexagenary characters.

Heaven's Heart: The Central Palace of the *Lo shu.*

Hetu: see *ho t'u.*

Hexagrams: the sixty-four figures formed by placing the eight trigrams on top of another in every possible combination. A figure made up of eight lines on top of one another, either broken or unbroken. The basis of the *I Ching.*

Ho hai: see *Huo Hai.*

Ho t'u: a square, like the *Lo shu*, used with the Former Heaven Sequence feng shui.

Hsia calendar: the traditional Chinese agricultural and solar calendar.

Hsien-sheng: a professional practitioner of feng shui.

Hsiu: the twenty-eight Chinese (uneven-sized) constellations or Mansions of the Moon, often found marked on one of the outer rings of a feng shui *lo p'an.*

Hsuan Kong: a school of feng shui that includes Flying Star feng shui.

Hsueh: the lair, or site of the maximum concentration of beneficial *ch'i.*

Hsun: the trigram of wind and early summer. Sometimes spelled "Sun."

Huo: Fire.

Huo Hai: the accidents and mishaps or mild bad luck location in a house.

I Ching: the Chinese "*Classic of Changes,*" a philosophical and divinatory book based on the sixty-four hexagrams.

Intercardinal points: NW, SW, NE, and SE.

K'an: the trigram of Moon and water and mid-winter.

Kan shih system: the sixty combinations of twelve Earthly Branches (*ti chih*) and ten Heavenly Stems (*t'ien shih*).

Kan-yu: an old name for feng shui.

Ken: the trigram of mountain and early spring.

Killing breath: see *sha ch'i.*

Kua: this character means both trigrams (three lines) and hexagrams (six lines).

Kua number: really the Annual Flying Star number derived from the year of birth of a male.

Kuei: ghosts; has been translated "demons."

K'un: the trigram of Earth and late summer.

Kwei: see *kuei.*

Landscape feng shui: see Form School feng shui.

Later Heaven Sequence: (*hou t'ien*) a circular arrangement of the eight trigrams, such that the trigram Ch'ien is in the NW. Used in assessment of the interior layout of homes or offices.

Li: the trigram of Fire and the south.

Li chun: the commencement of spring, the day the Annual Stars change, the beginning of the Chinese Solar New Year which begins on February 4/5 each year.

Liu sha: the six curses or "six imps" location in a house.

Lo p'an: the feng shui compass. The primary tool of feng shui.

Lo shu: the magic square with nine chambers (or Palaces), whose numbers add up to fifteen in every direction.

Luck: is considered to be comprised of three components known as Heaven Luck (fate), Earth Luck (feng shui), and Man Luck (your own efforts).

Lui sha: a common incorrect spelling of *liu sha*.

Lunar calendar: see calendar, lunar.

Lung: the Chinese dragon, a water creature, central to Chinese mythology and feng shui.

Lung mei: dragon veins, but definitely *not* the same as ley lines. They are the channels that *ch'i* follows through the earth.

Luo pan: see *lo p'an*.

Luoshu: see *Lo shu*.

Ming: life, fate, destiny.

Ming Dynasty: 1368–1644 AD.

Ming gua: see *ming kua*.

Ming kua: destiny trigram, or personal "*kua* number." Actually the Annual Flying Star of the year of birth, in the case of males.

Ming t'ang: "bright hall," the courtyard, or the open space in front of a building where beneficial *ch'i* can accumulate.

Mountain Star: the sitting star in Flying Star feng shui.

Mountains: The most important Ring on the *lo p'an* compass, which consists of the twelve Earthly Branches, eight of the Heavenly Stems and the four corner Trigrams. There are six Water, six Fire, six Wood, and six Metal directions on the twenty-four Mountains Ring.

MPW: Mountain-Period-Water order of stars.

MTW: Mountain-Time-Water order of stars.

Mu: Wood.

Nien yen: see *yen-nian.*

Pa chai: see Eight Mansion formula.

Pa kua: literally "eight trigrams," or more specifically, the octagonal arrangement of the eight trigrams.

Pa kua mirror: a mirror (flat, concave, or convex) surrounded by the eight trigrams in the Former Heaven Sequence designed to reflect *sha ch'i.*

Pa tzu: translates as Four Pillars, but literally means Eight (Chinese) Characters.

Palace: This is one of the nine *Lo shu* cells that a building is divided into for the purposes of a feng shui diagnosis. Each Palace (except the Central Palace) corresponds to one of the eight trigrams. Palaces are usually referred to by their trigram, i.e., the K'un Palace, or more simply by their compass direction.

Period: twenty-year period, nine of which make up a 180-year Great Cycle.

Poison arrows: see secret arrows.

Productive Cycle: the cycle of the five Elements that progresses: Wood, Fire, Earth, Metal, Water.

Qi: see *ch'i.*

Qing Dynasty: see Ch'ing Dynasty.

Reductive Cycle of the Elements: the five Elements reducing each other in the cycle order: Wood, Water, Metal, Earth, Fire.

Sam Sart: (Cantonese) see *san sha.*

San ban gua: see *san pan kua.*

San He: Three Combinations, a major traditional school of feng shui.

San pan kua: a configuration where all Palaces of the Flying Star chart contain the Mountain-Period-Water combinations of 147, 258, and 369, and there are no missing sectors. Reputedly, this structure is auspicious under all circumstances.

San sha: fate Stars called the three Evils or Three Killings, or literally the "three *sha.*"

San Yuan: Three Cycles, a major traditional school of compass feng shui.

San Yuan Chiu Yun: the three sub-cycles and nine periods.

Seam Needle: one of the directional needles on a San He *lo p'an.* The Heaven Plate reading of the outer Ring of twenty-four Mountains. The Seam Needle was originally used in yin house feng shui as the guideline to determine the influence of water, rivers, and lakes.

Secret arrows: cutting *ch'i* generated by a straight alignment of roads, trees, poles, or adjacent buildings.

Sector: an area of a room or building corresponding to one of the cardinal or intercardinal points, i.e., N, S, E, W, NW, SW, SE, NE.

Sexagenary combinations: The sixty combinations of twelve Earthly Branches and ten Heavenly Stems. Used also to identify the sixty-year cycle.

Sha: There are more than fifteen distinct and separate words/characters in Chinese, with different meanings, all of which can be transliterated into English as "*sha*." Even when they are pronounced with four different tones, many cannot be distinguished except by writing the Chinese character. There are three different *sha* relevant to feng shui:

> *Sha:* 殺 [first tone] killing, murder, slaughter, hence *sha ch'i,* "killing *ch'i*."

> *Sha:* 砂 [first tone also] sand (meaning man-made objects and small hills used as a geographical term), hence "the *sha* in front of a site."

> *Sha:* 煞 [fourth tone] as in the Fate Stars, the "three *shas*."

Sha ch'i: cutting or killing *ch'i.*

Sha qi: see *sha ch'i.*

Shan: mountain in the geographical sense, but also the specialist term for the twenty-four directions on the major *lo p'an* compass ring.

Shang: to ascend, up, above.

Shang shan hsia shui: literally "up the mountain and down the water," a reversed house chart.

Shar: see *sha.*

Sheng: life, growth.

Sheng ch'i: strong or generating *ch'i.* Success and great prosperity location in a house.

Sheng qi: see *sheng ch'i.*

Shui: water, also a general term for a river.

Sitting direction: where a house "sits," the opposite of the facing direction.

Sitting Star: see Mountain Star.

Solar calendar: see Calendar, solar.

Ssu ch'i: stagnant or torpid *ch'i.*

Stems: see Heavenly Stems.

Sun trigram: see Hsun.

Sung Dynasty: 960–1279 AD.

T'ai chi: the Great Ultimate from which everything else came. The "tadpole" symbol showing its division into yin and yang.

Tai Ji: see *t'ai chi.*

Taiji: see *t'ai chi.*

Tang Dynasty: 618–907 AD.

Tao: the Way, the essence of Taoism.

Taoism: the oldest of the three main religions of China: Buddhism, Confucianism, and Taoism. According to tradition, founded by Lao Tzu.

Ti: Earth.

Ti Shih: see Earthly Branches

T'ien: Heaven, or in one sense literally the sky.

T'ien i: see *t'ien-yi.*

T'ien kan: see Heavenly Stems.

T'ien-yi: the "Heavenly Doctor" or health location in a house.

Tiger, White: the Celestial Animal of the West.

Tong Shu: see *Tung Shu.*

Tortoise: see turtle.

Trigrams: the eight possible figures made of combinations of three lines, either yin (broken) or yang (whole) lines.

Tu: Earth.

Tui: the trigram representing lake and mid-fall/autumn.

Tung Shu: the annual Chinese Almanac.

Tung Sing: see *Tung Shu.*

Turtle or Tortoise: one of the four Celestial Animals, associated with the north. A yin creature often accompanied by a snake.

Tzu Wei Tou Shu: Purple Star system of Chinese Polar astrology, which has twelve Palaces and hundreds of Fate Stars.

Wang: prosperous, vigorous.

Water Star: the Star that corresponds with the facing direction, or front, of a house.

West Group: the people or houses whose best locations are NW, SW, W, and NE.

Wu Hsing: see Elements, five.

Wu kuei: the "five ghosts" location in house.

Wu xing: see *Wu Hsing.*

Wuxing: see *Wu Hsing.*

Yang: the active, male principle. Yang is the complimentary opposite of yin.

Yang chai: the houses of the living.

Yang Yun Sung: perhaps the greatest early master of the Form School of feng shui (840–c. 888 AD).

Yellow Emperor: Huang Ti (2697–2597 BC), perhaps the greatest of the legendary emperors. Not to be confused with Ch'in Shih Huang Ti (the first Ch'in emperor who "burnt the books" c. 221 BC).

Yen-nian: the longevity location in house.

Yi Jing: see *I Ching.*

Yin: female passive energy, the opposite of yang. Yin is used to characterize qualities such as dark, inside, negative, female.

Yin chai: literally "dark house," meaning tomb or gravesite.

Yin/Yang symbol: see *t'ai chi.*

Yu: space, geographical space.

Yuan: Period of twenty years.

Yun: literally "luck," the twenty-year Periods that repeat nine times in each 180-year Great Cycle. The Periods are called *ta yun*, the big luck; the annual cycles are called *hsiao yun*, the small luck.

Zhou Dynasty: see Chou Dynasty.

Zhou yi: an old name for the *I Ching*.

Zi wei: see *tzu wei tou shu:* a form of Chinese astrology, quite different from Four Pillar astrology.

Bibliography

BENNETT, STEVEN J. (1978). "Patterns of the sky and earth: the Chinese science of applied cosmology." In *Chinese Science,* vol. 3, pp. 1–26. University of Pennsylvania.

CHU, W. K. AND SHERRILL, W. A. *The Astrology of I Ching.* Routledge & Kegan Paul, London, 1976.

DE GROOT, J. J. M. *The Religious System of China,* Vol. 3, book I, part III, chapter XII, pp. 935–1056, Brill, Leiden, 1897.

DE KERMADEC, JEAN-MICHEL. (1983). *The Way to Chinese Astrology.* Unwin, London.

DORE, H. (1914 33). *Researches Into Chinese Superstition.* Trans. by M. Kennelly. Vol. IV, pp. 402–16. T'usewei Printing Press, Shanghai, 10 vols.

DY, VICTOR. *Feng Shui for Everybody.* Renaissance, Makati, 2000.

———. *The 4 Pillars of Fortune for Everybody.* Renaissance, Makati, 2001.

EDKINS, J. (1872). "Feng shui." In *Chinese Recorder and Missionary Journal,* Foochow, March.

EITEL, E. J. (1873). *Feng shui: or the Rudiments of Natural Science in China.* Trubner, London, reprinted Cokaygne, Cambridge, 1973.

FEUCHTWANG, STEPHAN D. R. (1974). *An Anthropological Analysis of Chinese Geomancy.* Vithagna, Laos.

FREEDMAN, MAURICE. (1966). *Chinese Lineage and Society: Fukien and Kwangtung.* Athlone, London.

———. (1969). "Geomancy." In *Proceedings of the Royal Anthropological Institute of Great Britain and Ireland* (1968 Presidential Address), pp. 5–18. Athlone, London.

HAYES, J. (1967). "Geomancy and the Village." In *Some Traditional Chinese Ideas and Conceptions in Hong Kong Social Life Today.* Hong Kong: Royal Asiatic Society (Hong Kong Branch), Hong Kong.

HSU, FRANCIS L. K. (1971). *Under the Ancestors' Shadow* (revised). Stanford University Press.

KAN, C. Y. (1968–69). "Feng Shui, its implications on Chinese Architecture," thesis, Hong Kong University.

KOH, VINCENT. *Basic Science of Feng Shui: a Handbook for Practitioners.* Asiapac, Singapore, 2003. *www.asiapacbooks.com.*

———. Hsia Calendar 1924 to 2024. Asiapac, Singapore, 1998. [Probably the first, and one of the clearest, Chinese Almanacs in English].

LEBRA, W. P. (1966). *Okinawan Religion: Belief, Ritual and Social Structure.* University of Hawaii Press, Honolulu.

LEGEZA, LASZLO. (1975). *Tao Magic: the Secret Language of Diagrams and Calligraphy.* Thames & Hudson, London.

LIP MONG HAR, EVELYN. (1979). *Chinese Geomancy.* Times Books International, Singapore.

LIPPELT, ULRICH WILHELM. *Feng Shui Demystified II.* AuthorHouse, 2004.

LO, RAYMOND. *3 Period and 3 Harmony Combined Lo Pan Interpretation.* [A manual accompanying Raymond's excellent English *lo p'an*]. Thompson House, Hong Kong, 2001. *www.fengshuicenter.com.hk.*

MARCH, ANDREW L. (1968). "An Appreciation of Chinese Geomancy." In *Journal of Asian Studies*, XXVII, pp. 253–67, February.

MARTEL, FRANÇOIS. (1971). "Analyse formelle de configurations symboliques chinoises." Diplome de l'Ecole Pratique des Hautes Etudes, Paris.

———. (1972). "Les boussoles divinatoires chinoises." In *Communications*, vol. 19, Paris.

MAYER, JEFFREY F. (1976). *Peking as a Sacred City.* Chinese Association for Folklore, Taipei.

MORAN, ELIZABETH, VAL BIKTASHEV, AND MASTER JOSEPH YU. *The Complete Idiot's Guide to Feng Shui.* (Foreword by Stephen Skinner.) Third Edition, Alpha Books, New York, 2002.

NEEDHAM, JOSEPH. (1956, 1959, 1962). *Science and Civilisation in China*: Vol. 2, History of Scientific Thought; Vol. 3, Mathematics and the Sciences of the Heavens and the Earth; Vol. 4, pt I, Physics. Cambridge University Press.

PALMER, MARTIN AND KWOK MAN HO. *T'ung Shu: the Ancient Chinese Almanac.* Rider, London, 1986.

RAWSON, PHILIP, AND L. LEGEZA. (1973). *Tao.* Thames & Hudson, London.

SHERRILL, W. A., AND W. K. CHU. (1977). *An Anthology of I Ching.* Routledge & Kegan Paul, London.

SKINNER, STEPHEN. *Divination by Geomancy: Terrestrial Astrology.* RKP, London, 1980 (new edition due out 2006).

————. *Feng Shui Before and After: Practical Room-by-Room Makeovers for Your House.* Tuttle Publishing, Boston, 2001.

————. *Feng Shui for Modern Living* (book). Cima/Cico Books, London and Trafalgar, New York, 2000.

————. *Feng Shui for Modern Living* (magazine). Thirty issues published by Centennial, London, 1997–2000.

————. *Feng Shui Style.* Periplus, Singapore 2003.

————. *Feng Shui, the Traditional Oriental Way.* Parragon, Bristol, 1997.

————. *Guide to the Feng Shui Compass.* Golden Hoard Press, Singapore and London, 2007.

————. *K.I.S.S. Guide to Feng Shui.* Dorling Kindersley, London and New York, 2001.

THAN, RICKY, AND RAYMOND LO *Chinese Almanac* (T'ung Shu) *for the Year of the Horse 2002.* Thompson House, Hong Kong, 2001. *www.fengshuicenter.com.hk.*

TOO, LILLIAN. *Applied Pa Kua and Lo Shu Feng Shui.* Konsep, Kuala Lumpur, 1993.

————. *The Complete Illustrated Guide to Feng Shui.* Element, Shaftesbury, 1996.

————. *Flying Star Feng Shui.* Element, London, 2002.

TWICKEN, DAVID. *Flying Star Feng Shui Made Easy.* Writers Club Press, San Jose, 2000.

WALTERS, DEREK. *Chinese Astrology.* Aquarian Press, London, 1987, reissued 2002. *[The most complete book on Chinese astrology available in English.]*

————. *Feng Shui.* Pagoda, London, 1988.

————. *The Feng Shui Handbook: A Practical Guide to Chinese Geomancy.* Aquarian Press, London, 1991.

WHEATLEY, PAUL. (1971). *The Pivot of the Four Quarters.* Aldine, Chicago.

WONG, EVA. *Feng Shui: The Ancient Wisdom of Harmonious Living for Modern Times.* Shambhala, London and Boston, 1996.

YAP, JOEY. *Ba Zi the Destiny Code.* JY Books, Kuala Lumpur, 2005.

————. *Feng Shui for Homebuyers: Exterior & Interior.* JY Books, Kuala Lumpur, 2006.

————. *Stories and Lessons on Feng Shui.* JY Books, Kuala Lumpur, 2005.

————. *The Ten Thousand Year Calendar: the Definitive Reference for Feng Shui and Chinese Astrology.* JY Books, Kuala Lumpur, 2004.

Feng shui software

Software for Feng Shui: see *www.fengshui-magazine.com.*

Sources of *lo p'ans*

You can purchase the Chinese compass, or *lo p'an,* in most large Chinatowns in cities like London, San Francisco, Kuala Lumpur, Singapore, and Sydney, or order via the internet from:

Dragon Gate, Kuala Lumpur, Malaysia.
www.dragon-gate.com.

Thompson House, Hong Kong.

Index

About the Author

STEPHEN SKINNER took his degree in English Literature and Geography, at Sydney University. Initially he worked as a Geography lecturer.

Research in Hong Kong in 1975 brought him in touch with local Chinese feng shui practitioners, where his skills with the theodolite complemented their interest in taking precise feng shui compass readings. This lead to Stephen writing the first English book on feng shui published in the twentieth century, the *Living Earth Manual of Feng Shui*, in 1976. This book is an updated reissue of that text.

When Western interest in feng shui began to be noticeable in the 1980s, Stephen produced a second feng shui book, *Feng Shui: the Traditional Oriental Way*, which became in 1997 an instant bestseller in the United Kingdom and has since gone into many editions.

In 1998 he launched *Feng Shui for Modern Living* magazine, whose first issue sold 121,000 copies per month, more than either *Elle Décor* or *Wallpaper* magazines in the UK. In 1999 he was nominated for PPA "Publisher of the Year" for his work in launching and publishing this magazine. This magazine helped popularize feng shui around the world, and it appeared in forty-one countries. Skinner even produced a Chinese-language edition in Taipei that ran successfully for thirty-four issues.

In the same year he launched the London International Feng Shui Conference, the largest feng shui conference ever held in the United Kingdom/Europe. The following year Stephen gave one of the three Doyle magazine lectures in New York, sharing the bill with representatives from *Martha Stewart Living* and *Country Living*.

Stephen has published a number of books on feng shui, including a book based on the magazine *Feng Shui for Modern Living*, *Feng Shui the Traditional Oriental Way*, *Keep it Simple Guide to Feng Shui*, *Feng Shui Before & After*, and the coffee-table book *Feng Shui Style*.

His recent work has included producing a card pack, the *Tibetan Oracle*, which utilized seventeenth century Tibetan manuscript sources to illustrate the Chinese sixty-year Animal and Element cycle. His interest in pushing back the frontiers of feng shui knowledge in the Western world has resulted in titles like *Flying Star Feng Shui* and his book on the lo p'an, *Guide to the Feng Shui Compass*.

Stephen Skinner is the author of over twenty books translated into more than twenty different languages. He currently lives in Johor Bahru, near Singapore, where he researches and does consultation in Singapore and around the region.

His website is www.SSkinner.com.